# I'VE GOTTA LITTLE BLACK BOOK WITH ME POEMS IN

## AND MORE

### JOHN E BATH

ISBN:9798652233617

*For my friend Ken*

# CONTENTS

# ACKNOWLEDGMENTS

My thanks to the following people for granting me permission to include some of their poems:

Jeremy Nash.

Muriel Buckingham (nee Hatchet)

Paul Asling

Peter Salter.

Lindsey Atkins.

Daley Slater.

Johnny Bonny.

Jane H Myers.

Pearl Street.

Stinky Daniels.

Lisa Galpun.

Henry James.

# ABOUT ME

*H*ello. Thank you for showing an interest in my little book of poems. I do hope you enjoy, at the very least, one or two of them, and who knows, you might also like one or two of the others. I hope to publish some more sometime in the not so distant near future.

The more perceptively, observant, eagle-eyed of you might pick up on the acrostic poems. As I am sure you are already aware, it means the first letter of each line, spells the title of the poem. (I Love You, Elvis RIP, That Dogs Face etc) See how many others you can find.

I have added a few that were written by some very dear, lifelong friends of mine. I'd like to take this opportunity to express my heartfelt thanks to them all for allowing me to include them. I have also added one which was penned by my lovely cousin Muriel. It is about her mum (my Aunty Vi) You will find I have actually included the Lyrics to a song of mine about my Aunty Vi, which I wrote some years ago. As for my poems, well, there are quite a lot of them. Some quite short, very short in fact, and some not so short.

They span over four decades, the earliest starting in 1977 after the tragic death of Elvis Presley. In no particular order, they are very personal to me, as I'm sure yours are to you too. I have also added a few more of my songs (minus the chord progressions)

London will always be close to my heart, in particular, Fulham. Having grown up there, I spent of lot of my childhood playing in Bishops Park and the Big Rec. They are just two, of many, of our great outside spaces, and I feel extremely privileged to have had the opportunity to make good use of them, and several other parks in this area, throughout my life. I come from a large extended family so, having lots of aunts and uncles, meant I also had lots of cousins to play with in my little street. (There were quite a lot of us living in Bayonne Road throughout the 1960s)

I am also fortunate enough to have shared the street with many great neighbours too. So all in all, I'd say I had the best childhood one could wish for. My love of Fulham, it's history and it's close knit communities, has had a huge influence in my writing over the years. There is so much more I would like to tell you about my family, my community and my life. But I'd better stop now. If I don't, I know I'll end up getting carried away, not for the first time. Of course, no poetry book (even one as modest as this humble contribution of mine) would be complete without mentioning the Genius of Wordsworth (Daffodils) - Houseman (Into My heart, an Air That Kills. How Clear, How Lovely Bright) or indeed, Rudyard Kipling. For that reason, I have decided to add the Kipling poem, 'If", at the back of this book.

I have included several small anecdotes of my own personal life experiences and a little extra local info too. I don't profess to be in any way an expert regards local history, and this is not an attempt at my trying to prove otherwise. There are already plenty of books covering that subject far better than I could ever wish to do. But I hope you might learn something, even if it's just a little bit, from my offering.

Of course, when it comes to doggerel versification, I need not remind you, there have been millions of poems penned by a salmagundi of peoples from all different walks of life, and many of them were written from a broken heart. I choose to be no different. Why should I be? But, in an attempt to add a little light to this darker side of life's tapestry, I have included some lighter moments here and there.

Once again, thank you for showing an interest in my work.

My very best wishes to you all, John.

~

# ELVIS RIP

*E*very day is a sad one,
  Living without him.
Very sad, to say the least,
In this world so grim.
So listen all you people,
Recite a prayer with me.
In time, he may be forgotten,
Please God, don't let that be.
©John E Bath

# HISTORY OF RICHMOND PARK

*L*ike most Londoners over the years, I have enjoyed many a summers day in the grounds of Richmond Park, with all it has to offer. I've had happy times there, and sad. I've spied on St Paul's cathedral through the telescope on King Henry's Mound. I've basked lakeside in the beautiful surroundings of Isabella's Plantation, and on the odd occasion, I've even fed the deer with a few treats (even though I know I shouldn't really have done so)

Here I've added a brief introduction to the Park. I hope you find it informative and interesting.

Richmond Park is London's largest royal park. It covers over 2500 acres. It was formed in 1637 when Charles the 1st enclosed the area as a royal hunting preserve. Even though the enclosure wasn't too popular at the time, the fact that the parkland was in royal ownership did prevent it from being swallowed up by the urban sprawl of London. Something, I'm sure you'll agree, we can all be truly thankful for.

Charles was really quite struck by the beauty of the grounds, and its possibilities as a hunting preserve. So much so, he moved his entire court to Richmond in 1625 to escape an outbreak of plague in London.

When he enclosed the park inside a stone wall he expressly allowed the public right of way. That decision proved to be rather important because in 1751, when Princess Amelia became ranger of Richmond Park, she immediately closed it to the public.

From then on, she, only allowed her close friends, or those granted special permits, to use it. The princess refused to listen to the disapproval of the public, but in 1758 a local brewer, by the name of John Lewis, was stopped from entering the park by a gatekeeper. Mr Lewis took the gate-keeper to court, and the court ruled in his favour, citing King Charles 1st's original intent to keep the park open. The princess was forced to lift her restrictions on entry, and the park has been open to the public ever since.

The park is known primarily for its woodland and grassland, but it is also home to thirty lakes and ponds. Among the latter are Pen Ponds, formed from ditches dug in the 1600s to drain the boggy ground. The Ponds were later used to raise carp for food.

## ISABELLA PLANTATION.

In the southern part of the park is a stunning 40-acre woodland garden within a larger 19th-century forest plantation. The most popular features of the Isabella Plantation are the evergreen Azaleas. They are at their best in late April and early May. Within the gardens are the National Collection of Wilson 50 Kurume Azaleas, which share the space with very large collections of camellias and rhododendrons.

## THE DEER PARK

Richmond Park is famous for its population of red and fallow deer, which have been allowed to roam freely throughout the park since 1637. The deer have played a large part in helping shape the landscape of the parkland, and their grazing helps maintain the grassland environment.

If you get the chance to walk through the park, have a look for the distinctive 'browse line' on the tree trunks, you can clearly see where deer have eaten all the twigs and leaves. They can reach up to a height of almost five feet. The deer engage in the annual 'rut', with male stags (red deer) and bucks (fallow deer) competing for females.

The young deer are born from May to July, and are often hidden in the long grass and bracken. Please be aware of this and whatever you do, do not approach young deer, or come between calfs and mothers.


**PEMBROKE LODGE**

At the highest point in Richmond Park is an elegant Georgian mansion named Pembroke Lodge. Once upon a time, it was a humble single-room cottage occupied by a 'mole-catcher.'

His job was to deal with the moles, whose molehills presented a danger to horsemen during hunts. It was later enlarged to provide a residence for a gamekeeper, who then in turn let it out to Elizabeth, Countess of Pembroke.

From 1788 the Countess of Pembroke called upon architects Sir John Soane and Henry Holland to transform the lodge into a fashionable residence. After the Countess died in 1831 King William IV granted the lodge to his son-in-law, the Earl of Erroll, who extended the house. Queen Victoria later gave it to John Russell, who served as her Prime Minister. The queen visited Lord Russell at Pembroke Lodge. His grandson, Bertrand Russell, the philosopher, grew up here.


**POETS CORNER**

Of course, I couldn't write about Richmond Park without mention of Poets Corner. It is situated just outside Pembroke Lodge Gardens. Once there, you will find a park bench donated by the family of the much missed 'Godfather' of punk, Ian Dury. He often took his children into the park to play. The back of the bench is inscribed with the title of one of Ian's songs, 'Reasons to be Cheerful'.

Nearby is a curved memorial seat commemorating James Thomson, an 18th century Scottish poet most famous for penning the lyrics of Rule Britannia! Thomson spent the last years of his life in Richmond. There is a black wooden memorial board to Thomson nearby. He died on the 27th of August 1748.

# THE BLUENESS OF THE SKY

*a*s I sit in Richmond park, the sun shines down.
　　It reminds me of you, and I start to frown.
The times we had, were full of fun.
But now all that's left, is me and the sun.


It's lonely in the park. But I ask myself, why?
　　And then I see the sun, up there in the sky.
　　Alone, I'm at the duckpond, throwing bits of bread.
　　Alone, I feed the Reindeer, wishing I was dead.


When we went to the park, we'd sit there through the day.
　　We'd listen to the radio, and we'd watch the children play.
　　But now I'm all alone, I feel I want to die.
　　And as I look up way above me,
　　I feel the blueness of the sky.
　　©Pearl Street

# YOU COW

*I*'m not ashamed to say I need you.
I'm not ashamed to say I care.
I thought someday, you'd come along.
But I never knew when, or where.

Since we started courting, a few weeks since,
I feel you don't want to know.
I need someone to care for.
Though I hadn't always let it show.

Now though, I've opened my heart to you.
And I've told you how I feel.
You act as if I mean nothing to you.
And it hurts me.
© John E Bath

# REINCARNATION

When I was a Lamb, I played in the field, With my mum, in the sun, through the day.

With her coat all shorn, she felt such a plum, once the spring had past our way.

We chewed on some grass, with her baldy mates, and we gathered together in flocks. They'd huddle and hide, trying not to be seen, looking all sheepish, minus their locks.


Our mad march friends had long since gone,
   on to pastures new and afar.
   Hopping and skipping and doing what they do,
   dodging the occasional car.
   The black and white Collie would find us at night,
   and escort us back to our Pens.
   Once we heard those strange whistles from farmer Jack,
   we knew the day was at an end.

The 'lucky' ones got to regrow their fleece,
    Not that they made a fuss.
    As for me and my mum, it wasn't to be,
    so I guess that's what happened to us.


Now we wait for divine intervention,
    to see what new life we will live.
    If its Human that's fine, but not an mp,
    most take out so much more than they give.


A poet would be good, or even a king,
    with a castle, a drawbridge and moat.
    But whatever human, we should grow up to be,
    when it's cold we'll wear a Sheepskin coat.
    © John E Bath

~

# A GIRL LIKE YOU (SONG)

*M*y names John, and I am single. But I'm not like Boy George.
My names John, and I am single. But I'm not like Freddy, or Elton John, Andy Bell, George Michael or William Tell, cause. my names John, and I am single, and I'm looking for a girl like you.

I've been single, for most of me life. Thinking I would never find a girl to be my wife, till that day when you walked by, and I saw you in the corner of my eye. My names John, and I weren't single. Cause I found a girl like you.

Well, there was the dancing and the prancing, and the kissing you, and missing you. The nights in, and the fighting. And the making up, and falling right back out again. And dancing in the rain, then we were making up again. It was driving me insane. My names John, so I stayed single. I didn't need a girl like you.

I prefer it when I live on me own. At least then, I get the chance to
use the telephone. When it rings, it rings for me. And I'm the only
one with a door key. My names John, and I'll stay single. Just my
three cats and me. That's Don, Vince and Harry. My names John and
I am single, I don't need a girl like you. Or you, or you or you or you
or you, or you, or you or you, you, or you, or you. You, or you or you,
or you, or you.
My names John, and I am single………….
But I'd like a girl like you.
© John E Bath

❧

# NONSENSE

*N*onsense. Nonsense, nonsense, nonsense, nonsense.
    Oh my, such nonsense.
Nonsense, nothing but nonsense.
So much nonsense.
Everywhere, nonsense.
Nonsense. Nonsense, nonsense, nonsense, nonsense.
So much nonsense.
Endless.
©Jeremy Nash

# HISTORY OF THE CRABTREE

*I*'ll never forget the very first time I went into the Crabtree for a night out. It was a Saturday. May the third to be precise, back in 1975. How do I know that after so many years have passed? Well, that's easy really as it was the night of the FA Cup final. Sadly my team lost two nil to West Ham. But at least we got to the final. That in itself was an amazing achievement. This led locally to a real carnival atmosphere, as was expressed by many of the houses, and streets in and around Fulham, by their having been decorated with Fulham flags, and bunting, of all shapes and sizes.

A shindig of much merriment, repeated just two years later with the addition of dozens of street parties, in celebration of her majesty's silver jubilee. You would have thought we'd won the match that day, what with all the celebrations that took place.

In Thomas Faulkners book, 'Fulham' c1813, he states that the village of 'Crabtree' took its name from a large crab-tree formerly growing there which stood near the public house known by that name.

In Charles Fèret's book, 'Fulham Old and New' c1900, he states that in ancient times Crabtree was 'an insignificant village consisting of half a dozen houses inhabited by gardeners, brick makers etc, together with a small inn.'

It's true that in 1666 the Parish Clerk listed only nine names as residents of Crabtree. In 1674 there were 23 and as late as 1739 only 14 were listed. In the 1760s the pub had been known as 'The Pot House' after a pottery operating in the area. It served the market gardens and was on the edge of the land of the last of the local farmers, Mr Edward Matyear.

It later changed its name to 'The Three Jolly Gardeners' and only later took the name of the area, being known ever since as The Crabtree. In 1817, a survey described the property as 'A picturesque old inn in front of which was a small open space enclosed from the river by a wall. Here a few seats were disposed for the use of customers.'

According to Fèret, an old willow tree grew there. Stating that, many years earlier, an ingenious landlord had adopted the idea of converting the willows shady branches into a bower; in the midst of which he arranged a table and some seats. Apparently, the access to this area was via a flight of steps. By 1895 it had evidently became a popular haunt with the locals. Back then, there were several pubs along the riverside, but the Crabtree is the only Fulham one to survive.

To the north was the Maltings, established about 1790 by Mr Joseph Attersoll and to the south stood Belle Vue, a house built c1816 for John and Thomas Scott. Subsequent owners included John Thomas Edwards, a dentist and a man of somewhat eccentric habits, apparently keeping a wolf at Belle Vue. In 1872 it was taken by Henry Poole of Savile Row and later became the property of Messrs Mears of Crabtree Wharf. The new Crabtree pub was rebuilt in 1898. It was on the same site as before, adjacent to the river, being next to a 'beach' and overhung by a willow tree.

It was much bigger than the previous building and had pretensions as a hotel. Containing a spacious billiard room and a large room available for concerts and public meetings.

When Edward Matyear died in 1910, he left the whole of the residue of his estate to King Edward VII's Hospital Fund who sold it on to local developers 'Allen and Norris'. Not far from the Crabtree is Nella Road. Nella being 'Allen' written backwards. Building work began on the 'Crabtree Lane Estate' the following year. The Crabtree Pub was soon to be in the centre of a very populated area.

After Edwards funeral, the mourners were conveyed to the Crabtree Farm where his will was read. It contained legacies of £500 each to the West London Hospital and the Lygen Almhouses. £250 to the sisters of Nazareth. £500 five hundred pounds each to the five cousins. £100 each to Misses Good (three), £20 each for three nieces, £50 to Mr. Thomas Matyear, £50 to Mr. Thomas Matyear's brother, now in Canada, £100 to Mr. Jeremiah O'Brian (the deceased's foreman) £100 to his housekeeper, Mrs. Young. £20 to his carman, Mr Harry Carter, and a month's wages to all his employees who had been in his service for twelve months at his death. As I mentioned earlier, the residue of his land, valued in 1910 at around sixty thousand pounds, was devoted to King Edward VII's Hospital Fund. All the legacies were free from death duties.

(Aberdeen Evening Express 14th October 1910)

# THE CRABTREE

'*A*fternoon John, back on the beers?'
  'Hello, Phil, gotta light mate,? Cheers.'
Smoke fills the air, people chat.
Murphy sips his Guinness, alone in his Trilby hat.
Their cigarettes, making more smoke.
Joggers with their orange juice, complain as they choke.


'Anyone for tennis? hwa, hwa, hwa'.
  Hoo-Ray Henries, la-di-da.
  The losing streak is teasing, Mabel and her purse.
  With a handful of coins, she tries her best, to beat this dreaded curse.


Ching, ching, ching. At last, the machine pays out.
  Eyeing up her winnings, sips excitedly at her stout.
  'Hello Giles, sorry I'm late, I couldn't get away.'
  Who is this girl? she looks great, bit outta MY league, I'd say.

'Money or love?' asks the man playing Pool.
   'Money? you having a laugh?
   Then quietly replying, 'love,' said he.
   'You know I'm not that daft.'


A man in a suit, pays his bill.
   'Thank you Flo, that was a splendid meal.'
   'Don't forget your brolly, sir.
   Do come again.'
   Outside it's cold.
   And pouring with rain.


The girl bids farewell,
   the office workers, gone.
   Several people stay behind,
   including Phil and John.


More coins are swallowed,
   it's another win for Mabel.
   Phil agrees to a game with Frank,
   who's setting the up the table.


But as another cigarette is lit.
   There's not much left to say.
   For all the people left behind.
   It's just another day.
   © John E Bath

# I LOVE YOU

*I*f I were born in an earlier age.
      London wouldn't be the same.
Once upon a time, the place was mad,
Victorian times, insane.
Eventually though, things would improve,
Yesteryear would be in the past.
Only, now our future, could be short and sweet.
Unless, we make it last.
©John E Bath

# CHELTENHAM TERRACE

*M*any years ago, way back in the 1920s, my Great Aunt Eva married a Welsh gentleman named Bob. They bought a quaint 'cottage type' house together in Bridgend. It was one of those lovely little terraced, two up-two down, houses, in a little side street by the name of, Cheltenham Terrace. As children, in the 1960s, my sisters, parents, grandparents and I spent a week there with Eva during the summer for our annual holidays. We were lucky enough that our dad had his own car, a second, or third hand, Ford Consul. Oh boy, was I forever getting car-sick in it. I can still remember the registration number, 406LRT, Getting there was never a problem, and parking was a doddle as there were so few privately owned vehicles back then. I don't ever remember meeting great Uncle Bob though, so I guess he must have died before I was born.

As was the case for most of us back then, they had an outside toilet. It was a damp, dark, creepy little outbuilding with flaking paint which clung desperately to the faded old whitewashed walls. It was quite a spider magnet. The filthy, antiquated high level cistern, draped in its mass of thick cobwebs afforded me no reason to feel any different. One particular memory I have of it is from when I was around six years old. I went into the toilet, and looking up at the cobwebs, I had a somewhat uneasy feeling of the 'hee-bee gee-bees'.

In dire need of the toilet, I dropped my Khaki shorts and sat myself down onto the cold, weathered wooden seat. I'd only been sat there for about a minute when this huge great spider quickly shot out from behind the toilet. It stopped right next to my right foot which made me let out a really loud scream. I immediately pushed the door open and flew out of the loo, still with my shorts around my ankles. My parents and grandparents must have wondered what on earth was happening as they had come out from the kitchen and were coming to my rescue. They did their best to try to calm me but I was terrified.

I don't know how they managed to get me to use that toilet after that, but they did. I assume they must have gone in there and given it a thoroughly good clean out beforehand. To this day I hate outside loos. In fact, I can't bare to be near any sort of damp, dark nooks and crannies, especially those accompanied with the obligatory webs infestations.

Most days we'd travel to the coast at Porthcawl where, once the tide was out, we would climb down the rock cliffs to the beach, and quietly explore the rock pools. Then we would make our way back up the cliff face and have a picnic on the grass verge, followed with some gentle physical games to burn off the calories.

At the end of the day, we would usually take home with us an early evening 'chip shop' supper, consisting of Rock, Cod, Saveloy, Chicken, three large portions of chips, Gherkins and pickled onions. If we were lucky and they had them, we'd get lots of batter scraps too, or as us old 'stick in the mud, Cockerneys' like to call it, 'crackling'. Soon after us kids went to bed, the evening was, more often than not, finished off with the grown ups sat at the table, usually playing Newmarket for an hour or two, before they too retired to bed.
© John E Bath

≈

# ANOTHER FOUR PENNIES ARE PUT INTO IN THE POT

The waves lap at the edge of the beach, the
tide is out, the sea water is very cold, the beach
is full of rock pools and dad points out the tiny little fishes and baby
crabs going about their 'temporarily restricted' morning.
The water is warm in there, we watch, but do not
disturb.

The cliff face is 20 or 30 feet high in places
but is like Everest to a 5 year olds eyes.
There are lawned areas atop the mountain which
lay next to the South coast road.
Mum and Nan are sitting with Gt Aunt Eva on a blanket having
been busy preparing the picnic, Ham sandwiches and Lemonade
powder. The radio is on, I can hear 'Excerpt from a Teenage Opera'.
Granddad is shouting encouragement to my
sisters who are playing bat and ball.

All too soon, the sun is setting, there is a slight chill in the air.
Everything is carefully wrapped up and placed in
the boot of dads Ford Consul as we set about
heading to the Chippy.

The little terraced house has old furniture mostly
made of wood, well built and sturdy. There are
very few cars in the street, parking is no problem.

The table looks lonely as it watches us all seated
on the slightly more comfy chairs eating our food from the
newspaper it was served in, Nan burps, Grandad
says 'Pardon', and I giggle as he gives me a cheeky wink.

There is an outside toilet with a huge spider as a
sitting tenant, she likes to come out to say hello
when I'm sitting there, albeit briefly, as I don't
hang around.

It is dark, it's night time, I'm off to bed and I imagine
the table smiling now as Mum, Dad, Nan and Grandad
are sitting at it playing Newmarket, 'Red'!, no Red Mick?… Harry ?
Another four pennies are put into the pot as my tired eyes
decide to close for the night.
I wake up, I'm 60 years old, they are all gone, Gt Aunt Eva, Mum,
Dad, Nan and Granddad, even the table, but the house
still stands.
I often wonder who lives there now.

© John E Bath

# MONDAY

or the third consecutive day, the thundering midday rain beat violently against the bedroom window, drawing her attention, once more, to the harsh, cold-ness of the outside world as it did so.

She couldn't help but feel that, somehow, maybe she would have been far better off had she not bothered to debunk from the lonely solitude of her plump, snuggly 'thirteen tog' duvet draped futon, and stayed in bed till the evening.

But she was up now, so she bravely followed her nose as it guided her downstairs towards the putrid smells emanating from the previous nights exiguous victuals.

Stumbling her way in shear anticipation of the vortex of the new dawn, or noon as the case was here, she heard the late delivery of yet more bills as they dropped in through the snappy, stainless steel letter-box. As she made her way to the kitchen, she bent down and picked up the small, part drenched, offending pile of yet to be opened correspondence, and semi-consciously threw it onto the table. In doing so, she knocked her redundant engagement ring, which had been sitting there for ever, against the fragile, smear stained glass bowl disturbing some blackened, badly bruised, long forgotten, squidgy Bananas in the process.

From out of the corner of her astigmatic right eye, she noticed the washing up bowl full of the 'unclean' from the past week. She dug out a teaspoon of hardened, instant coffee from the jar and tipped the contents into her one remaining clean mug. On it, the words 'TEA-TIME' were now so faded, they were barely visible, almost unreadable. But at least it was clean. The ancient, scaled up kettle seemed to take ages to boil, and as it was doing so she wondered if she should do some toast. Well, she was in the kitchen anyway so it seemed like a good idea at the time.

Her off white, tired old fridge (which she'd unaffectionately named Smeghan) complete with its complement of abundant dirty finger prints, loudly hummed its usual buzzy tune in the corner of the room. Having just switched on the radio, thanks to the arial being long since snapped off, she heard the weak, dulcet tones of, 'You're So Vain' constantly fading in and out. Add to that, the fridges dodgy old motor interfering with the signal, well, that didn't help none.

Almost void of any contents, Smeghan just about afforded her the measly offerings of an out of date jar of olives, a tepid, unopened carton of sour milk and an almost empty tub of overly soft, far too liquidy, easily spreadable, dairy free margarine. Tucked right at the back on the middle shelf stood a, 'used just once,' long forgotten jar of plum jam, with its all too familiar science project fermenting within the sanctuary of its glass encasement.

All of this made it no less tragic that the bread was stale. Annabel poured the recently boiled water from the kettle into her midday beverage and escorted it to the table. Stubbing her naked little toe on the leg of a chair on the way there, and just managing to not drop the bowl of brown sugar all over the floor,

'Fuck it,' she said, and went back to bed.

©John E Bath

~

## THE BIN, THE THIGH AND THE LAMPPOST

I like coffee,
I like tea.
I like life,
I like thighs.
I like eyes,
Eyes like me.
Eyes like you.
Eyes so blue,
Eyes don't know,
what to do,
without you.
©Pearl Street

# HISTORY OF BISHOPS PARK

*S*ir John Hutton, Chairman of the LCC formally opened Bishops Park in 1893. The park included land known as Bishop's Walk, Bishop's Meadow and West Meadow which were conveyed by the Ecclesiastical Commissioners, as Lords of the Manor of Fulham, to the Fulham District Board of Works on the condition that the land should be laid out and maintained as a public recreation ground.

The Meadows had already been protected from flooding by the creation of an embankment. In addition, the river wall was built by Joseph Mears between 1889 and 1893.

The park was extended in 1894 prior to opening in 1900, by the inclusion of Pryor's Bank and its gardens. Although the house (then called Vine cottage) was demolished in 1897, the old gardens were preserved. The gardens contain stone figure sculptures depicting "Adoration", " Protection", " Grief" and "Leda", presented by the sculptor J Wedgewood. A further sculpture "Affection", a mother and child by Herman Cawthorn was added in 1963.

The grounds of Fulham Palace, from 16th century one of the most important botanical Gardens in London; obtaining national and international significance and under Bishop Compton, who moved to the palace in 1685. With the aid of George London, the most renowned and skilled gardener of his day, the collection was embellished in 17th century with many exotic species including tulip, walnut and maple trees and a cork oak. Seeds and plants came from collectors in the American Colonies, India and North America.

This tradition of collecting continued in 18th century when Bishop Porteous planted several cedars and into 19th century when Bishop Blomfield planted deciduous cypress and ailanthus. Roque's Map of 1741-45 shows the Palace to have been surrounded by formal gardens. They were replaced by landscaped grounds c.1770. The moat, which surrounded the Palace, was filled in 1921-24; archaeological excavations have shown that it had its origins in pre–Saxon defences.

# BISHOPS PARK (SONG)

The day that you confessed to me.
            About the way things are, and how you should be free.
Of all the pain and sadness that you feel.
I'd never hurt you girl, and I remember still.
The memory of that night we first kissed.
Sat in Bishops Park, freezing in the mist.


Oh now, look what you've gone and done.
    You put my heart down in my shoes, and made me fear the sun.
    Cause when it shines, it takes me back in time.
    To that perfect day when you were mine.


But once again, I'm all alone. Feeling sad and blue,
    hoping you might telephone.
    And as I sit and watch tv. I get the feeling you,
    were wishing you were here with me.

Oh now, look what you've gone and done.
  You put my heart down in my shoes, and made me fear the sun.
  Cause when it shines, it takes me back in time.
  To that perfect day when you were mine.


And as another day begins. I get the feeling you,
  are lying once again, with him.
  So I sit here all alone.
  © John E Bath

# GROANS ONE

*I* went out with a tennis player for a while but I packed her in as love meant nothing to her.

~

Even though I'm losing my hair, I still have my old comb. I just can't part with it.

~

I got a job on the dust years ago. I was told there wasn't any special training involved. They said I'd pick things up as I went along.

~

Never criticise someone until you have walked a mile in their shoes. That way, when you criticise them, you'll be a mile away, and you'll have their shoes.

~

If too much wine can damage your short term memory; imagine what too much wine can do.

∾

If I had 50p for every maths test I failed, I'd have £6:38.

∾

Why did the scarecrow win the noble peace prize? Because he was out standing in his field.

∾

Women only call me ugly until they find out how much money I make as an author. Then they call me ugly and poor.

∾

A roman legionnaire walks into a bar, holds up two fingers and says, 'Five beers, please.'

∾

Just say NO to drugs. But, to be fair, if you're talking to your drugs… You've probably already said yes.

∾

I like rice. Rice is great when you are hungry, and you want two thousand of something.
    ©John E Bath

∾

# WHO KNEW?

*A*s exclusive as Fulham is nowadays, in the 16<sup>th</sup> century, people would flock to Fulham mainly for late night gambling and drinking.

North End Road market moved to Fulham in the 1880s. Lining the road with stalls ranging from food to materials to beauty products and, even though it may have changed a great deal in recent years, it is still as popular now as it was back then.

The grade I listed Fulham Palace was home to the Bishops of London and it is said that the building was lived in for potentially 500 years. It is now looked after by the Fulham Trust and the general public have access to the building as well as the exquisite Botanical Gardens.

The prestigious Peterborough Estate houses just off the New Kings Road were sold in the late 19<sup>th</sup> century for a mere £300. Nowadays the prices of these beautiful red brick family homes exceed £3million.

It is said that J. Nichols ordered ten times too many sandstone lions for the estate meaning each house adorns one and also shares one with each neighbour.

Did you know that there are over 1500 stone lions to be found in the borough of Hammersmith and Fulham meaning it is has more than any other borough after City of Westminster?

~

The Hurlingham Club is an exclusive sports and social club set on 42 acres of land. However to have access to it you will have to be a guest of a member as there is a 50 year waiting list!

~

The Kings Road was originally built for the royal family to have an easy route out of London and then later on Fulham Road was built so that the King could move freely and secretly.

~

Close to the junction of Parsons Green Lane and Fulham Road, opposite Kelvedon Road, is the carriage entrance to Park House, which stands in Parson's Green Lane. A stone tablet let into one of the piers of the gateway is inscribed, 'Purser's Cross, 7th August, 1738.' This date refers to the death of a highwayman which occurred here, and of which the London Magazine gave the following particulars:

'A highwayman, having committed several robberies on Finchley Common, was followed to Mayfair, where he thought he would be safe, but he was quickly discovered at a public house in Burlington Gardens, refreshing himself and his horse. However, he had time to re-mount, and rode through Hyde Park in which there were several gentlemen's servants exercising their horses, who, taking the alarm, pursued him to Fulham Fields. Once there, and finding no probability of escaping, he threw money among some country people who were working in the fields (much of Fulham was agricultural back then)

He told them they would soon witness the demise of an unfortunate man. He had no sooner spoke these words when he pulled out a pistol, pressed it to his ear, and shot himself, before his pursuers had a chance to stop him. The coroner's inquest brought in their verdict, and he was buried near that junction, with a stake through him; but it was not known who he was. It is highly probable that his remains are still there somewhere, under the cross-roads.

∽

Fulham Broadway station was originally named Walham Green station, however in 1952 local resident won the battle to change the name to Fulham Broadway? Kinda wish he'd kept his mouth shut to be honest.
© John E Bath

∽

# IT REMINDS ME OF ME

There's a feather on the floor.
It's lying, all alone.
It reminds me, of me.
© John E Bath

# YOU

*A* love so precious, a love so true, a love that comes from me to you.

You're my love, my soul, my happiness.

You're the stars in my sky, you're the reason I try.

You're my strength, my heartache, my pain, you're my world, my everything.

You're the one who dictates my feelings,

the one who knows my fears.

Together forever and never to part.

You're all I need.

©Paul Asling

# CAN'T YOU SEE IT IN MY EYES

*I* don't know if you want to know.
I don't know if you know, I want to know.
But I know I want you to know, I want to know.
So, how do I let you know, I want you to know, I
want you to know, I want to know?
'Cause I don't know.
Can't You See it in My Eyes?
© John E Bath

# TINY DANCER

*D*ance was all that was needed,
  to fill her day with joy.
But she felt sad, as she danced alone,
there was something missing, a boy.


Daley watched her from the junior team,
  Then got promoted, into her group.
  From that day on, they danced together,
  till he pushed her face in her soup.
©Daley Slater

# MERRY CHRISTMAS MS LAWRENCE

*W*ay back in the olden days of 1988, I was living in Bermondsey, south London. I was working as a courier driver. My parents were living in Fulham. They'd lived there all of their lives, as did their parents and their parents parents before them. Not long before that, around the mid 19th century, most of Fulham was farms and fields with some rather grand manor houses dotted about here and there, some of which still exist today. Although not actually acting in their original capacity, they are no less beautiful in their architecture and design.

One or two are now schools and at least one of them had been used, for many years, as a British Legion social club. That was until recently (2010) as I now believe that one has been sold and will revert to its former glory in the not so distant future. The re-gentrification of Fulham being almost complete.

I wasn't so fortunate as to have the opportunity befall me to make Fulham my place of residence as an adult. That's not to say I didn't want to live there as it was never my intention of living anywhere else. When I was about 26, I made an appointment with the housing department at the council offices to get myself registered on the housing waiting list.

A few days later, I arrived at the office with about about thirty minutes to spare. I always prefer to be early, as opposed to late, when attending appointments as I find it quite stressful when the clock is ticking and I get delayed by one thing or another, and if there's one thing London is almost always guaranteed to offer up on a regular basis, that is, delays on it' s roads.

I introduced myself to the security guy in the reception area and explained I was there to see a certain Ms Lawrence at my specified time (midday if my memory serves me correctly) He took down my details and instructed me to take a seat and said someone would come to see me in due course. I then sat and waited, along with many other people who were there for a whole variety of reasons.

After waiting for just a short while, I was approached by Ms Lawrence. A not too unattractive, hippyish looking woman with long frizzy brown, borderline ginger, hair. Not much older than I was at the time, she wore an autumnal coloured tie dye tee shirt and maxi length, wrap around skirt, she invited me to take a seat at her desk to take down all the necessary info regards my application. Once she was satisfied she had documented all the information she required of me, she made it perfectly clear I would be at the back of a very long queue.

I said I understood and I even expressed to her my sympathy with the pressure her department was under. Our meeting was concluded by my briefly explaining to her how I was educated in Fulham, and that my parents, my grandparents and even some of my Great-Grandparents had all grown up and lived there. I also mentioned about how, since leaving school some nine years earlier, I was working for Hammersmith and Fulham Council, having done my apprenticeship with them as a plumber, and I dearly wished to live locally to my mum and dad. She told me I needed to acquire at least thirty points to qualify for housing. Not once, did she inform me as to how one actually achieves this magic number.

However, I did later learn, from another source, that I would get one point for every five years I'd lived in the borough. That meant I had a shortfall of twenty five points. Anyway, having opened my heart to her about my predicament, she coldly looked at me and said, and I quote, 'I don't believe just because someone is born somewhere, that gives them the right to live there.' Well, you could have knocked me down with a feather. 'Blimey,' I thought. 'She's a barrel of laughs. With friends like her, who needs enemies.' To say I was quite taken aback at this remark, would have been an understatement.

Now, at this point, I want to make it perfectly clear that I'm not the sort of person who makes 'demands.' Never have been, never will be. I just really, really wanted to live in the place where my mum could pop in to see me, the place where I knew lots of people, the place where I felt I was a part of something, the place where I felt I actually belonged. I can't quite put down in words how shattered I felt upon hearing her say that. Neither, for that matter can I write down in words, my response to this eye watering revelation of hers. Suffice to say, I think she may have been reasonably irked with my response, which I took careful consideration to express, in as politely, but no less remorselessly brutal a fashion, as I could muster.

So, after somehow managing to get myself on the housing waiting list without the instigation of the onset of world war three, I duly left the premises and popped into my local for a swift half. As I sat sunning myself in the beer garden supping my afternoon tipple, my mind drifted back to the time when, at one point in my life, back in the very early 1980's, for a period of just over a year, when I squatted in several unoccupied council flats and houses in and around Fulham.

Thanks to my friend Terry, the first one I stayed in was down a little side street off of the Dawes Road. Well it was one of two actually as it was a terraced house, with a flat downstairs, and another upstairs. The downstairs flat had been purposefully vandalised by the council (one of the genuine rarities they were consistently good at) In doing so they had rendered it quite uninhabitable.

They'd taken out more than half of the floorboards. They had even smashed the bath and basin and most of the plaster had been removed from the walls, leaving them with the bare, dirty, brickwork.

So, considering my faute de mieux, I plumped for the second flat with Terry, upstairs. I moved into the spare bedroom of that one, and being as it was getting near Christmas, I bought an artificial tree, decorated it with the obligatory baubles etc and proudly displayed it in the living room window at the front of the house. I finished off my yuletide embellishments by writing the words 'Merry Xmas' in large letters on the window using that spray on snow which comes in pressurised canisters.

I had been in and out of 'digs' before that, and for a couple of days before I started squatting, I actually had to spend two nights sleeping rough in my car. The day after, what was to be my final, car camping adventure, Terry said I could have a room in his squat. And that is how I came to be there. I had been there less than a week when I set about laying down a bit of carpet. I installed a gas cooker, and a gas fire, and I furnished the flat with a nice double bed (I do like my creature comforts) And I even managed to find a couple of comfy chairs for the lounge.

After about four months had passed the council had somehow got wind of our occupancy and when I got home from work one night (yes I was working at the time) the council had been and stuck lots of warning letters all over the front door informing us to expect the bailiffs to call in two weeks time to remove me, Terry and all of our belongings. My cousin had a furniture business around the corner from us and he had a nice large box van. I asked him for his help and he happily obliged us by letting me and Terry put all our things in the van overnight the day before they were due to come. The next morning, at around 9am, Terry and I sat in my car opposite the flat.

We sat and watched them as they, not noticing us sitting there observing them, walked straight in through the opened front door of the now empty flats. We'd removed the both of the locks the night before and still had them in our possession. Terry had previously wedged one of the backroom windows tightly shut and, once the bailiffs were satisfied that we'd vacated the premises, we saw them put a new Yale type lock on the main front door and off they went.

As soon as the coast was clear, Terry got out of the car and made his way around to the back and removed the wedge in the window whereupon he made his entrance. Two minutes later, there he was, standing at the front door with a big grin on his face. We unloaded the stuff from my cousins van, replaced our locks and promptly moved our belongings and ourselves straight back in. Now I felt a small sense of security once again as I knew I could be there for at least another four months. Not ideal, but better than sleeping rough in my car.

This was around march and Christmas had long gone. For some reason, even though I had put the Christmas tree away, I never cleaned off the 'Merry Xmas' message I'd sprayed in the window. Over the coming weeks Terry had met, and rather fallen in love with a girl from Roehampton. She had her own flat there, and as time progressed I saw less and less of him as he, quite understandably, stayed with the new love of his life. But I carried on squatting all the same.

Some months later the council returned and did their usual thing and plastered another lot of their little warning letters all over the front door so I contacted a friend of mine who worked for the council. His main job was to clear out the houses and flats when the previous occupants had vacated the premises for whatever reason.

He took me to a flat he had recently cleared just up the road a bit from this one and, with the help from a couple of other mates, I moved into that one. I went to the local electricity showroom and got the electrics switched on as they had not long been disconnected.

I lived there for several more months, paying the bills, till that very same thing happened once again and I had just two weeks to get out. My friend from the council told me of a three storey town house that was empty just a quarter of a mile away from where I was staying. It was one of many newish properties that had been built on the site of the demolished streets where I grew up as a kid, and where my mum and her family had grown up too.

We went there with my special skeleton key, I say skeleton key, it was actually a very large screwdriver which, with some gentle persuasion, would more often that not open any closed door you might chance upon. There was no need for it though as the door of the new premises wasn't even locked so in I went and quickly put my lock on the door and closed it shut, I was safe again, for a while at least.

A couple of years or so later, around 1985, my circumstances had changed considerably and I was no longer squatting. After several visits to the council I was eventually offered a flat of my own, but sadly not in my beloved Fulham. I would have been a fool to have turned it down though so, even though it was 0ver 15 miles away from my desired location, I moved in and finally had a home of my very own.

Fast forward to 1988 at the Blue (Bermondsey) Having lived here for some time, I carried on working as a gas engineer for about one more year, then I packed it in and started to work as a mini-cab driver.

It gave me a great opportunity, one that would mean I could keep myself connected to Fulham. I managed to get a job with a cab firm there and, even though as each shift came to an end and I went home, I was still far away from my home town, at least it kept me in frequent contact with my family and friends.

Several months had passed when, on one particular, uneventful night, I had to pick up a passenger from the road I originally squatted in with Terry. As I passed my old squat I glanced up at the window and I saw, to my amazement, the words 'Merry Xmas' still sprayed there on the glass of the upstairs living room window. It was mid summer, so I knew it wasn't a Christmas message from a new occupant. I couldn't help but feel a bit sad knowing it was my old message, as it was at least two years since I had vacated it for the last time. Was it really possible that the flat had remained empty for all that time?

A few months went by and I found myself taking another passenger through that road once again. I slowed down as I approached my old squat and, as I looked up at the window, there it was in all it's glory. I pointed out my Merry Xmas message to them and they were, under-standably, quite shocked when I explained I wrote it, by now, nearly three years earlier.

Then, over the following few years, with the message still there for all to see, I made it my job to always point it out to my passengers if by chance it was on our route. Another year passed, then another and another. It was there each and every time I passed it till one day, over twelve years after I had first written it, it was finally gone and a new tenant had moved into the flat.

Much water has passed under many bridges since those days, and a lot of life changing experiences have occurred. Terry married the girl from Roehampton and had a couple of kids with her. My parents have both passed on and are no longer here. I achieved many things over the years, and I recently moved out to the sticks where I have finally retired from the constant bobbing and weaving, ducking and diving, of the rat race.

It was just a small gesture on my part, now nearly forty years ago, to wish passers by a Merry Xmas but, for me at least, it left a lifetime legacy regards how I had witnessed first hand how dire mismanagement can affect peoples lives. I have very little doubt that this would have affected many other people in one way or another. It certainly made an impact on me. I can only hope things may have improved a bit by now, even if just a little. But I won't hold my breath.

Merry Christmas, Ms Lawrence, wherever you are. I hope you have many more.

©Jeremy Nash

# PARTY OF FRIVOLITY

Oh to be Jocular, Irresponsible or Foolish,
or to be Infantile, by the seaside at Dawlish.
Oh to act Childish, Trivial and Giddy,
to be Flippantly, Self Indulgent,
like an innocent kiddy.
To be Fluttery, Playful even Lighthearted.
To be sure to Giggle,
when someone has farted.
To be Exuberent and Fruity, and Daffy and Sappy.
It's best to be Frivolous, and always be Happy.
Fatuous, Foolhardy, Non-sensical, Inane.
To be Thoughtless, Witless, even Hare-brained.
To be adequately Inconsequential, in pursuit of a Laugh.
To be any of these, it's easy, be Daft.
©John E Bath

# MY POND

*A*s I sat relaxing beside my pond late last night, I became pleasantly aware of my blissful extrication from the madness of the world outside. Reclining my steamer amidst the abundance of Sunflowers and Grasses of my little garden sanctuary, I lay back into it, and as I did so, the softness of the cushions caressed my back and sides, affording me a most agreeable sense of warm embracement.

I briefly thought about the capriciousness of the previous weeks whimsical experiences, when all of a sudden I found myself quite ensorcelled by the sound of the running water cascading down the little falls. Then my eyes focussed on the copiousness of stars high up in the paradisiacal sky amidst the ever expanding black curtain of eternity.

Contentedly, I smiled to myself when, quite out of the blue, my harmonious tranquility was interrupted by a police car as it raced by the end of my road. Its lights dancing in the darkness of night, all skipping and jumping as if they were tippy toes, and its sirens performed a duetted plethora of fortissimo musical notes that appeared to amuse themselves for what I yearned to be hours, but in fact it was just a few seconds.

Then fading into the distance, their lights dimmed long before the sound of the sirens.

As they did so I thought to myself,

you noisy git.

©John E Bath

~

# HAPPY FATHERS DAY

To Dad,
I let you down, so many times,
so many years ago.
But you stood by me, through thick and thin,
you and Mum always let me know,
that I was your son and you loved me lots,
more than words could ever say.
And the mistakes I make, make only once,
and soon, I would find my way.


Now the years have passed so quickly,
and I miss you more each day.
I have almost all I dreamed for,
but I'd give it all away,
if we could be together, on a warm and sunny day,
like the times we went to Runnymede,
where we'd sit and eat and play.

But what I have are memories,
of the bestest sort around.
The bestest sort of memories,
that ever could be found,
of the bestest Mum and the bestest Dad
and the bestest childhood years.
And I've the bestest ever girlfriend
and to you we both say cheers......
© John E Bath

# HAPPY BIRTHDAY GEORGE

*B*ack in the early part of the 1990s
a life long friend of my family, George
Foster, was about to celebrate his 86th birthday. His
eyesight was all but gone and he struggled to get
about unaided. I bought him a card and penned this
little ditty for him…….

Your time is passing by now.
 You're not as young as last year.
 All the same, today's your birthday.
 And I'm glad to see you're still here.
 I know you eyes ain't what they were.
 And you've joined those that walk with
 white sticks.
 I just hope your hearing, isn't quite so bad.
 After all, you are eighty six.
 © John E Bath

# HUMMING BIRD

*T*here is one bird, I'd really love to see.
     It's tiny in size, not much bigger than a bee.
It flaps its wings, as fast as a flies,
But isn't equipped, with quite so many eyes.


It'll feed from your hand, if you offer it some treats.
   But, silent in nature, you'll not hear it tweet
   It'll hover right before you, It'll hover high and low.
   And you'll hear it's wings a buzzing, then it's time for it to go.


Alas, I've never seen one, but I know that they exist.
   And I'll always keep, at the very top, of my 'must do' bucket list,
   The first chance that befalls me, to put down in written word,
   Of the day I held, in the palm of my hand, the beautiful Humming
Bird.
   ©John E Bath

# THE MIRROR/LOVE

$\mathcal{W}$hen you get what you want in your struggle for self.
And the world makes you king for a day.
Just go to a mirror, and look at yourself.
And see what that man has to say.


For it isn't your father or mother or wife,
Whose judgement upon you must pass.
The person whose verdict counts most in your life,
Is the one staring back from the glass.


He's the fella to please, never mind all the rest.
For he's with you right up to the end.
And you've passed your most dangerous, difficult test.
If the man in the glass is your friend.
©Johnny Bonny

Love….

Love is a feeling,
  A very funny feeling.
  A feeling that you've rarely felt before.
  A feeling that you feel,
  when you feel you want to feel.
  That feeling, forever more.
  ©Johnny Bonny

# I SAW A PAINTING, SO FINE AND SO RARE

*S*ee the busy bee being
       busy by the bathroom
bidet bowl.
Big bloody deal,
bollock brains.
© John E Bath

# SUIT YOURSELF

*H*er: 'I've gone back to him, John.
        I'm sorry.'


Me, failing miserably at trying to
    act with lackadaisical indifference:


'Suit yourself.'
    © John E Bath

# YOU SAID

*D*o you remember when you said we could
all holiday abroad?
We didn't, did we!
Do you remember when you said we could
all go to Brighton for the weekend?
We didn't, did we!
Do you remember when you said we could
all live together?
We didn't did we?
Do you remember when you said you'd never
go back to him?
You did, didn't you!
© John E Bath

# MUM

My mother's name is Violet, though everyone calls her Vi.
She's a very hardworking person, don't think she will ever retire.
Her children go to see her, Not often as they should.
But you know how children are, Not always very good.

There are seven of us children, Our partners, our children too.
There are our children's children also, So you see, there's quite a few.
But nothing's too much for her, She lays on a very good spread.
She cooks a big roast dinner, To make sure we're all well fed.

She's always cheerful looking, With a smile upon her face.
Sometimes she must be very tired, But never shows a trace.
So, thank you mum for what you are, For all that you have done.
Your children love you, oh so much. That's why we call you mum.
©Muriel Buckingham (nee' Hatchet)

# LIVIN ON MY OWN (SONG)

*G*etting used, to living on my own, once again.
　　No more sorrow, no heartache, no tears, no more pain.
　　But the days can be so hard and cruel.
When you face them on your own.
Then the evenings, feel so lonely.
Watching tv, staying in and eating all alone.


Getting used, to living on my own, once again.
　　But tomorrow, the sun won't shine, and there'll
　　be lots of rain. And I guess I'll do the same old
　　thing. No doubt, I'll try to pass the blame.
　　No more mobile, conversations, costing fortunes,
　　knowing you, will always be the same.
　　Getting used, to living on my own, once again.
　　©John E Bath

# WEDNESDAY

or the fifth consecutive day, the midday rain beat against the bedroom window, albeit, a tad less violently this time. Once again, it drew her attention to the harsh, cold-ness of the outside world as it did so.

She couldn't help but feel that, somehow, maybe she would have been far better off had she not bothered to debunk from the lonely solitude of her plump, snuggly 'thirteen tog' duvet draped futon, and stayed in bed till the evening.

But she was up now, so she bravely followed her nose as it guided her downstairs towards the, rather pleasing smells, emanating from the previous nights amuse-bouche, and suchlike.

Stumbling her way in shear anticipation of the vortex of the new morning, or noon as the case was once again, she was pleasantly surprised to see the snappy, stainless steel letterbox had nothing but a Pizza menu to throw at her. She made her way to the kitchen expecting the Bananas to be, by now, completely black. She knew she daren't pick them up for fear of them leaking their insides all over the table. But as she got there she noticed the fruit bowl had been replenished with three Apples, three Bananas and two Pears, all fresh.

Finding this a somewhat refreshing, even if totally unexpected, change, it was ever so slightly marred as, once again, she saw her redundant engagement ring sadly resting up against the sugar bowl.

She stood there staring blankly at the wall for several seconds. From out of the corner of her 'minus five diopter' left eye, she noticed the sink was completely clear of any unclean plates or cutlery. Even her old 'Tea Time' mug was missing from the bowl, which was empty of any contents, including the usual, cold, dirty old, washing up water.

Her attention was again drawn to the cupboard, she opened the door to find there was a brand new mug on the shelf in front of her. All clean and shiny it was. It was next to a jar of fresh, unopened, instant coffee. She removed the mug from the cupboard and placed it next to the kettle, dug out a teaspoon of soft, fresh, instant coffee from the, nope opened, jar and spooned the contents into it. On it, the words 'COFFEE-TIME' were clear for all to see. The ancient, scaled up kettle had somehow been replaced with a nice new, metallic red one, which took no time at all to boil. As it was doing so, she wondered if she should do some toast. Well, she was in the kitchen anyway so it seemed like a good idea at the time.

Her off white, tired old fridge (which still went by the name of Smeghan), quietly hummed a gentle tune in the corner of the room. This time though, its complement of abundant dirty finger prints had all but disappeared. She switched the radio on, and thanks to the arial having been refitted, she heard the dulcet tones of, 'You're So Vain' playing loud and clear, without any distortion whatsoever.

Stocked full of a multitude of contents, Smeghan afforded her a generous offering of, a fresh jar of olives, a cold, unopened carton of fresh milk and a new tub of easily spreadable, dairy free margarine.

This made it all the more pleasant when she found that the bread was fresh. Annabel poured the recently boiled water from the kettle into her midday beverage and escorted it to the table. Stubbing her naked little toe on the leg of a chair on the way there, and just managing to not drop the bowl of brown sugar all over the floor, she woke up with a start, to find it was all just a dream.

'Fuck it,' she said, and stayed in bed.

©John E Bath

⌇

## GROANS TWO

*I* was kidnapped by a mime artiste once. I can't talk about it though as he did unspeakable things to me.

~

Some people say I'm self centred. But enough about them.

~

I bought myself a pen that can write upside down. It can write lots of other words as well.

~

My wife asked me to put Ketchup on the shopping list. Now she's complaining because she can't read the shopping list.

~

How do you get two whales in a mini? Drive west on the M4.

~

My mate has a magic dog. He's a Labracadabrador.

~

You've got to hand it to my mate, Dave. It takes a lot of balls to play golf like he does.

~

They say we shouldn't eat at night. If that's the case, why do they put a light in the fridge?

~

A ventriloquist is performing with his dummy on his lap. He starts to tell a dumb blonde joke when a young platinum-haired beauty jumps to her feet to protest. 'What gives you the right to stereotype blondes that way?'

Flustered, the ventriloquist begins to apologise. 'You keep out of this!' She yells. 'I'm talking to that idiot on you knee.'

~

Every book is a children's book when the child can read.

~

Feminism is not a fad. I mean, it's not like 'Angry Birds' Although it does involve a lot of er…..anyway, moving on.

~

I had glasses at 11, tooth braces at 13. I said to my mum and dad, 'Lets not leave it there. How about a hearing aid? I'm thinking of chatting to a girl for the first time in my life and I want as much corrective apparatus on my head as possible. I think that's what women like.'

∼

Trains in the UK can be late for all sorts of reasons: Speed restrictions, livestock on the tracks, or a totally substandard rail infrastructure that's publicly funded, privately run and answerable to no one. All sorts of reasons.

∼

I recently downloaded this new app. It's great, it tells you what clothes to wear, what food to eat and it lets you know if you are overweight. It's called the Daily Mail.

∼

I was gonna write a joke about time travel. But what's the point, you lot didn't laugh anyway.

∼

Instead of calling my toilet the 'John,' I call it the 'Jim.' That way it sounds better when I say I go to the Jim every morning.

∼

An Englishman, an Irishman and a Scotsman walk into a pub. The barman says, 'Is this some kind of a joke?'

∼

# THE BACHELOR

*H*ad you been born a boy,
      I would have shed a hundred tears.
Had you been born a girl,
I'd take on all your darkest fears.
I would have loved to see you walking,
for the first time in your life.
And hear you call out 'Daddy',
in the arms of my dear wife.

To see your face at Xmas,
when you opened up your toys.
And see you go to big school,
with the bigger girls and boys.
Then when you found rebellion,
driving mum and me quite luny,
I'd like to have seen the back of you,
as you headed off to Uni.

As you studied hard and partied hard,
    then earned you first degree.
    I'd love to have seen your face again,
    as you showed it to mum and me.
    With your first proper job,
    and your first proper wage,
    and your first proper home of your own.
    We'd meet your first proper lover,
    and wait till the seed had been sown.

    On the day before the wedding,
    you'd drink goodbye to being alone.
    We'd see in your eyes,
    as we said our goodbyes,
    the love you'd always known.


Then, as we heard the first cries of your baby,
    we'd look back at our lives and we'd say.
    Was it good what we did,
    in the lives we have lived.
    Did we do, what we could, the right way.


But some of us never had children,
    and some never wore a gold band.
    Some of us regret letting chance after chance,
    foolishly slip through our hands.
    As for me, I'm now in my 60's,
    and I'm happy with the life I've had.
    But one thing still hurts,
    having loved mostly flirts,
    is knowing I was never a dad.
    © Jeremy Nash

# WHO'S THE BRIGHTEST

*M*irror, mirror, on
the ceiling.
Well: not everyone has it
on the wall.
©Lisa Galpun

# FAIRY TALES

My walls had trains and boats and planes,
    papered from ceiling to floor.
My bed was by a window,
Half open, half shut, was my door.
I laid in my room with my tired eyes,
while the sun was still aglow.
Then the Blackbird sang me lullabies,
till the Moon began to show.


I never slept alone in my bed,
    my dreams were with me too.
But they died there, every morning,
as I'm sure they did for you.
So, off I went to another place,
where fairy tales came true.
And all my toys would come alive,
and we'd play the whole night through.

Then as I awoke many years had passed,
  or at least thats how it seems.
  For I wondered why life, wasn't quite the way,
  it was in all my dreams.


The trains and planes upon my wall,
  with the boats have long since gone.
  I'm older and grey, with joints that ache,
  but my heart keeps beating on.


So all I can say to the people that dare,
  to try for what they want to achieve.
  Don't doubt the things, you want to be,
  in yourself you must believe, 'cause,


If fairy tales, are fairy tales,
  and fairy tales come true.
  Then fairy tales, aren't fairy tales,
  to the likes of me and you.
  ©John E Bath

~

# DEBBIE HARRY

*I*'ll never forget that day in 1978 where I gave Debbie Harry a couple of poems I'd written. It was in the middle of September, the sixteenth to be precise, and if my memory serves me correctly, it was a Saturday. She and her band, Blondie, had played a gig at the Hammersmith Odeon that afternoon and my mate Martin and I thought we'd try our luck at getting to see Debbie and the band as they left the building. We made our way around the side of the building to where the stage door was. We thought we might get lucky and see her at the door, but as we were on our way there, we passed the huge roller door at the back. It's where the roadies loaded and unloaded the gear.

The door was fully open and people were coming and going with various items of musical equipment. I noticed a black bin liner by the entrance to the backstage area of the theatre. It was full of old scraps of paper and other such rubbish. I impulsively picked it up and carried it in with me, in the hope the people there might think I was one of the workers. It worked. I found myself walking across the stage with this bag in my hand, followed closely behind by Martin.

Thanks to it only containing paper and cardboard, it wasn't too heavy to lug around. I looked out across to where the audience would be, being careful not to trip over the huge amount of cables strewn across the, at this moment in time, fairly deserted stage. 'Well, this is a first,' I thought. I felt quite honoured to be able to see the view from this particular perspective. I've lost count the amount of times when, as a child, I'd sat with all the other kids looking in 'towards' the stage when we went to the Saturday morning pictures there throughout the 1960's. And here I was, looking 'out' from it, towards the seating arena.

I carried on to the other side of the stage and, now that it had served it's purpose, I placed the bag down by a couple of others that appeared to be waiting their turn to be taken out. We made our way backstage and came across several more people who were chatting amongst each other. No one was taking any notice of us so I carried on with my exploration. I soon discovered a staircase and made my way up to the next floor. I saw a door with a sign on it that simply said the words 'Bands Room'.

I tapped on the door but got no answer so I opened it and went in. I remember seeing a holdall on one of the chairs but made no attempt to look into it. It was, after all, someones property, but I did see a can of Special Brew Lager. It was half empty but I picked it up to keep as a sort of souvenir. We left the room, returned to the stairs and went back down. As we made our way through yet another door, I noticed an open area about the size of a large foyer. I noticed it had a small bar with a man standing behind it serving drinks. There was an official looking man in a smart blazer, standing to the side of it. He appeared to be politely guiding people in their various duties and made mention of their having a refreshment once they were done. I approached the bar and went to walk past it when he looked over to me and spoke.

'Have you had a drink yet, son?' He asked.

Holding up my can of beer I cheekily answered,

'Yes, I'm alright John, I've got one here'.

He didn't seem to mind my brazenness and took little notice as Martin and I walked off to see where we could go next.

A few minutes later, we found ourselves in a longish corridor. There were about seven people lined up standing along the wall of this corridor. They were quietly talking amongst themselves so I stood by the man at the end. I took out my packet of cigarettes and offered him one which he accepted. I never asked his name, or what he was doing, and we spoke briefly about something or other of little importance.

Just then, Debbie Harry appeared from the other end of the corridor and walked towards where I was standing. She stopped and spoke to the man that I was just smoking with and verbally gave him a phone number with which he could contact her on. I couldn't believe it. Debbie Harry was standing right next to me.

Sadly, she never spoke to me, I doubt she even noticed me, and she made her way back along the corridor. Then she disappeared into her dressing room further down on the right hand side. I had the idea that, if I were to make my way to that end, I would be outside her dressing room. The people there all seemed far too busy talking about this and that to notice as my friend Martin and I made our way there.

Standing outside, quietly chatting with Martin, the door opened and a man said 'Ok, folks, that's enough for now, miss Harry would like to get changed.' A man and a woman came out from the dressing room and left. I assume they were from the New Musical Express or Melody Maker and were doing a short interview. There was I, standing outside Debbie Harrys dressing room, the door was wide open and no one was taking a blind bit of notice of my being there.

As I looked into the room I saw two basins. Once again impulse took over and I went in and started to wash my hands. I thought if I did that, I would at least be in the same room as her. It seemed like a good idea at the time, and it worked. I was surprised to see how small the room was, and as I was washing my hands I looked to my right and there she was, not three feet away, looking into a mirror removing her make-up.

She looked at me as I glanced across to her. I asked her to take my two poems to read later. 'Would you do me a favour, please. Just take these poems and read them,' said I, all sheepish. 'Just take them and read them?' she asked, in her adorable, American drawl. Looking back, I wish I'd just asked her to sign them and give them straight back to me. Isn't hindsight a wonderful thing. For some strange reason, I started to walk backwards as I left her dressing room. I'm not quite sure why I walked backwards. I assume it was to continue to see her for as long as I possibly could before making good my escape.

Just then, I heard the voice of the man who originally asked the journalists to leave, as he asked me 'Have you got your backstage pass?' He soon realised I didn't have one and showed me the exit and escorted me off the premises. As I looked back to him, I noticed the sign above the door. It was the Stage Door.

So, as surprised as I was, I did at least eventually get to go through it, but from the inside/out and not, as I would have expected, from the outside/in.

I kept that old beer can for a couple of years after that, till one day, my mum was cleaning out my bedroom. She thought it was rubbish and threw it out.

©John E Bath

~

## THE LIFE AND TIMES OF WHYMMS OLIVIA BASKING III'S WINDOW

*S*o smooth, so fine.
     So clear and so brittle.
So flat, so thin and so shiny.
So fragile, so steady.
So generous and kind.
So sharp, so blunt and yet,
so, unpredictable.
©John E Bath

# CHANGES

*C*hanges. Changes, changes, changes, changes, changes.
   How come there are so many changes.
Always changes.
Never ending, changes.
Got to be changes.
Everywhere, changes.
Sod it.
©Jeremy Nash

# DO HELP YOURSELF TO AN APPLE IF YOU WANT ONE

The constant writing in books.
Bitchy girls, giving deathly looks.
The teachers snidey, without a doubt.
All we can think about, is home and out.
Many late nights, not coming home.
Waking in the morning, too tired to come.
All we do, is graft for nothing, kidding
our parents, we're learning something.
Not any day, has anything in store.
Life in this hell place, is only a bore.
One day I'll crack, and get out of this place.
Find straight people, that ain't two faced.
All I want is to never stop running.
To live in this world, you have to be cunning.
The trouble is, there's no one to turn to.
Only people that laugh, behind you.
But as I get older, I'll have a life full of knowledge.
The day I can run, and say goodbye to this college.
© Lindsey Atkins

# MORRISONS BAKED BEANS

*A* couple of weeks ago, Thursday week past to be precise, we went shopping at Morrisons ( oh yes, nothing but the best for us ) and I'd heard about the baked beans offer of a 4 pack for 79p instead of the usual price of £2.79. Well, I thought, make the best of a good thing and buy 10 packs. That should see me through till November. When we got to Morrisons I rushed to the baked bean section only to discover the shelf was completely empty, grrr.

I caught up with Shaz and told her about my dire misfortune and she lovingly sympathised with me, flourishing me with the compassionate tenderness only she can compassionately and tenderly flourish me with, in a compassionate, tender sort of way.

A couple of days later Sharon decided to confess to me that she did in fact see a huge display of the said item piled up in a different section and took it upon herself, at the time, to not to tell me (I cant think why)

Sharon : 'John I must confess, I did see a huge amount of baked beans piled up in a different section and took it upon myself not to tell you'

(See, I told you so)


Well, this week when we went shopping, I checked out the baked beans and the offer had changed as it was £1.00 for a '4 pack'. Still not wanting to miss out on a good thing a found there was still a few left and I managed to purchase five '4 packs'.


Sharon was delighted, so much so she's promised me I can spend the next few weeks camping out in the garden shed...

How exciting :-)

© John E Bath


~

# WORLD WAR TWO

*E*ighty years ago yesterday, Germany, not just 'some Germans', as certain people would say today, but GERMANY, invaded Poland.

Eighty years ago today, my folks were somewhat anxious as to what might happen as the First World War had ended just 21 years earlier.

I can't begin to imagine quite how my people were feeling at the time, but they were made of much stronger material than many of today's spoiled, entitled lot. They were British, proppa British. Bulldog British. Full of the old Dunkirk spirit. They were made of the right stuff, and were preparing themselves for round two.

Knowing war was almost certainly on the cards, and readying themselves to knuckle down and 'get on with it,' yet again, I imagine they were feeling a bit miffed.

Eighty years ago tomorrow, they got the answer that was not necessarily the one they were hoping for and, once again they were at war with Germany. I imagine my folks put the kettle on, made a pot of tea, sat at the table and quietly said 'Bastards !'

©John E Bath 02-09-19

# WHAT'S HIS NAME?

*S*treetlights beam,
        through pools of darkness.
The streets of London are silent,
as if the city had been evacuated.


A figure all bent and black,
    came and stood beside me.
    I ask, where are you going?
    He told me he didn't know.
    I asked him where he's from.
    He answered, who wants to know?


For a moment,
    I felt his breath.
    He spoke in a whisper,
    I am Death, can you not see?
    I told him,

I am not coming with you.
     Pull me all you want,
     but I will fight you all the way.


Staggering away,
     his hair receding and grey,
     he fades into the distance.
     Wanting to run,
     back to my youth,
     with its laughter and fun.
     Memories from the past,
     flash through my head,
     and I ask myself,
     where did I go wrong?
     ©Paul Asling

∽

# I THOUGHT YOU WERE SUPPOSED TO WEAR IT AROUND YOUR NECK

*L*ook at that fellow, over there by the bar.
    He's got greased back hair, a leather jacket
    and a scar.
He's got an earring in one ear, and a tie
wrapped round his forehead.
That's strange, I thought you were supposed
to wear it around your neck.
© John E Bath

# MORE TIMES

More times gone.
      Predictable, I never wished for.
Tedious for some, but life goes on.
More times have gone.
Years rolling past.
Millions of heroes, it'll never last.


More times gone.
   Contentment, a vanishing dream.
   More times gone.
   A repetitive theme.
   More times gone.
   Forever slowly ticking.
   © Peter Salter

# VINCENT

As I sat looking up at the Harvest Moon tonight, it dawned on me it
might not be too dissimilar to a kind of bus stop, a Lunar bus stop if you
will. The one where you got the bus to the stars, and then on to infinity;
the place where all the love goes.
The main difference being, you didn't catch the bus, it caught you, at the
time of your most final, incorporeal fall. And, when you see a 'full' moon,
it meant the bus was ready for its next journey. Don't be sad when it's
gone as there will always be another one, and another, and another,
always.

Sometimes, when someone special to you is onboard, the moon shines extra bright, just for you. Tonight, the moon was shining extra bright and was beaming long after its 'Harvest' time. That particular moon has gone now, as has Vincent with it, to the stars and beyond. It will be back though, to catch us too when it's our time.

© John E Bath

~

# INTERLUDE: WALKING ON THE DECK OF THE TITANIC.

*W*ell, that was quite an undertaking. You actually made the effort and took time out of your invaluable lives to read all those poems, when there are so many, nigh on indisputably, better things for you to occupy your leisure time with, wow. Thank you, seriously, from the bottom of my heart, thank you. It is more appreciated than you could ever know xx

So, for that reason, as a means of a mild dose of diversification. For those of you that have come this far before stashing this book in the shadows. You know, that bit at the back of your, 'rarely gone to' shelf, which is the sort of place most of us forget we even have. The sort of place where it's so dark, you could store 'recently harvested' potatoes for months on end, and they would still be as fresh as they were from the day you first put them there. The sort of place where the book would be fated to, dare I say it, to be pushed to the back, never again to be seen for millennia, well, centuries, well decades, well ages anyway.

So, for that reason, as a means of a mild dose of diversification, how about a bit of a break from all that poeticisationalising. Are you ready for that? Good, then I shall begin. About thirty five years ago I got my very first landline phone. It was rented form BT as were many house phones back then. It had a small monochrome display which, when I lifted the receiver and started to dial, the number I dialled came up on the screen.

I had the idea that it might be good thing if, when someone phoned you, their number would show up on the little screen, giving you the option if you wanted to take the call, or not, as the case may be. I did nothing with my idea and a few years later, it became commonplace, as we still see to this day.

Not long after that, I had the idea of a doorbell answering machine. I suggested it to a few people, most of which said they would be concerned that an undesirable person would know you were out and, well you can guess the rest. I said that you didn't need to let anyone know if you were in, or out. I explained that it simply meant you couldn't come to the door just yet.

And, if we go back a few years before that, to the time when many people started to have telephone answering machines installed. It didn't assist bad people looking up your name and address in the phone book, then phoning you up and, once no one answered the call, breaking into your home as, it wasn't necessarily indicative of your being at home or not. Again, I did nothing with that idea.

I still think too much at times. I have several other idea floating around in me bonce. One of which has had many people laughing at me (not for the first time I can tell you) after I mention it, but I think it's certainly worth considering. All it needs is an interested billionaire like Branson, Musk or Bezos. Are you keen to read more? Jolly good, I shall continue.

Imagine if you will, a 600ft floating, reinforced, stainless steel bowl. A bowl this size, once it has been towed out into the Atlantic Ocean, can be turned upside down, sunk, and ever so carefully placed over the remains of the Bow section of the Titanic, two miles down on the seabed. The Titanic was roughly 883 feet in length but broke into two separate pieces. The stern section being around 392 long and the bow section 491.

Now, having towed this 600ft 'bowl' over the site of the wreckage and placed it over the bow section, the water pressure should be more than enough to create an airtight seal on the seabed. With the right amount of equipment, and an airlock entry point pre installed at the bottom, and on the side, of the bowl (now in situ it will resemble a huge dome, not unlike the O2 in my beloved London) After pumping the water out of the dome, using machinery etc from the ship above the site, air could be pumped into it, again from above.

Once this had been successfully completed, with a continual supply of fresh air, or Helium, it might just be possible to create an area fit for humans to safely roam the site. It should also be possible to pilot a submersible which could make repeated journeys in taking two, or even three, expert 'Titanicolgists' down to the wreckage, and once docked onto the airlock entry point, they could safely enter the dome and walk freely amongst the wreckage. There, I've said it. Now you can laugh at me too. But hey, I can take it. He who dares, and all that 8-)

ps; I forgot to mention my 'non stop generating electricity generating device' using perpetual motion. It would contribute hugely in saving the planet from the madness of humanity's selfish destruction. Mr, Dyson, are you there? Oh well, maybe next time, if there is one.

©John E Bath

~

# LEARNING TO FLY

*S*at in my van waiting for the first job of the day, I was browsing through the pages of 'Loot' when I noticed an advert on the back page; 'Would you like to do a 'Loop-de-Loop' for charity, for free.' It was for the Mind foundation. I wondered if I'd like to give it a go but knowing my fear of heights might set me back I gave it a miss. The following week, there it was again. This time, it was on the front page.

This was in the days of the rising popularity of the new fangled computer video games industry. Namely the Sega Meagdrive, and the Commodore 64, with it's cassette attachment on which to load the games individually. Thinking back, some of those games could take up to twenty minutes to load, and once you played the first level, you had to wait another twenty minutes for the second level to load. Some of the levels took just ten or fifteen minutes to complete, or fail. Either way you had to start all over again, and so it continued. Patience, was golden rule number one of the day. Then came the amazing Atari 520-STFM with its side loading floppy disk with which to load the games. Thankfully, the games on the 520-STFM loaded a lot quicker than the C64 cassette system. Having bought all three of these consoles a little while after their release (I had to wait a few months for the cost to drop a bit as they were quite pricey at first) and being as I played on them regularly, I accumulated quite a collection of games.

I found the Sega Megadrive the best for playing golf on. A very addictive game it was too. Many visiting friends would play a round or two with me on that one. But it soon become apparent that most of the games I played on the C64 and Atari 520-STFM were flight simulators. They seemed to be the sort of games I was most interested in.

A friend of mine, Phil, introduced me to the C64. He was big into sports and most of his games were sport themed. I popped in to see him one day and as I said I'd bought a new game he said, 'Don't tell me, it's another flight simulator. Without realising it before then, it was true. All my games were flight simulators.

The first one I bought was for the C64. To say it was basic would be an understatement of the highest order. But even though the graphics were almost non existent, I persevered until I could 'take off, fly to a destination and, once there, safely land.' I bought two flight simulators for the Atari. One of them simply involved flying a small Cessna from one airfield to another, the second one was a jet fighter plane simulator. I mastered both to a fairly competent level. I remember taking my Atari to a friends place in south east London. He had the same console so we hooked them up to two of his televisions. Facing them 'back to back', he sat opposite me and we set off on a jolly jaunt across the 'English coun-tryside'. I was amazed to see him flying his plane next to mine on my TV screen, he was equally amazed in seeing my plane flying alongside him on his. This was groundbreaking stuff back then. We soon loaded the jet fighter simulator and it took no time at all for me to shoot him down (sorry Mark)

One day, while sitting waiting for a pick up, I got the call on my radio to go to Camberley. This was to collect a parcel, and deliver it back to the office I was parked outside in Greek Street, in the west end of London. By the time I got to the office in Camberley, I found they had closed for dinner. I found a phone box as my radio didn't cover that sort of distance, and informed my boss. There were no mobiles in them days. He said to stay in the area and find something to eat and wait until they were open. I decided to see if I could find cousin Terry's address, in Yately. I was hoping to pop in and say hello. On the way there I noticed a small airfield to my left, so I parked safely at the side of the road to see the planes. I dearly wanted to see one either taking off, landing, or both.

Nothing was happening so after about twenty minutes I started the van to continue towards Yately. As I set off, I reached the entrance to the airfield, which I soon discovered was, Blackbush Aerodrome. I stopped outside and pondered on whether or not I should dare to drive in. As I waited, a memory came flooding back to me from many years earlier. I was on an eight day, intensive driving course, all paid for by my employers at the time, the North Thames Gas Board.

There were usually three of us in the vehicle, two of us learners, and the driving instructor. Each day we would drive out of the gasworks at Bromley by Bow, and drive around several of the many quiet back streets. Once we had reached a certain standard, we were taken onto some of the more, how can I put it, busier of the roads. Then one day, I had the pleasure of driving on a country lane where the speed limit was sixty mph. I was allowed to drive at around fifty six mph. It was quite a thrill driving at that speed, and after a few miles the instructor suggested we pop into this little airfield he was familiar with, near a place called Ongar.

It's not that we just happened to pass it, as I'm more than convinced he had every intention of us going there. We went in and bought ourselves some refreshments. He couldn't wait to tell us how rich the owner was and, pointing out to some of the little planes through the window of the restaurant he seemed to get great pleasure in informing us, in no uncertain terms, 'You'll never get to be flying one of those. You could never afford it.' And here I was, all these years later, at the entrance of an airfield, contemplating on whether or not I should enquire about learning to fly.

'Shall I go in,' I thought. Thinking I would be immediately told to leave, I put on my 'brave, who dares wins' hat and drove in. No one came out to shoo me away. No one said, 'You can't park there, son. This is private land.' In fact, no one showed up at all. I looked across to the flying school. 'Blackbush School of Flying.' I got out of my van and made my way to the entrance. Nervously, I opened the door and was met by a Mr Robinson, or John, as he preferred to be addressed. He was most welcoming, and soon put me at ease. I found myself enquiring about learning to fly.

I never thought for one minute that I'd be able to afford it, but I soon learned that by making a few small sacrifices, it was doable. I even surprised myself as I started to ask him several sensible, almost intelligent, for me anyway, questions.

All too soon, I noticed the time had flown by (sorry) I thanked John, and made my way back to pick up the parcel and continued with my day. Sadly, I never did get to see my cousin for a surprise visit, but the next day, as soon as the newsagent had opened, I bought the latest edition of Loot. There it was, the advert I was looking for, once again emblazoned across the front page. I made some enquiries, and within a week they sent me a form with the conditions, and some advice as to how to obtain the sponsorship money for the charity. For the following few weeks I drove everyone mad. At work, down the pub, in the cafe. But to my surprise, every single person I approached, signed up to donate a pound here or a couple of pounds there. In next to no time I had enough sponsorship money to take part in this acrobatic, flight of a lifetime.

To better prepare myself for this soon to arrive, once in a lifetime, exciting adventure, I decided to book a two hour pleasure flight at a near-by airfield. I'd never been up in a small plane before, so it seemed like the sensible thing to do. In fact, I'd only ever flown once, and that was to Spain and back some years earlier. My mum, dad, sister and brother in-law came with me to Biggin Hill in Kent where, having made ourselves known, we were introduced to a certain young man by the name of Capt. Pittock.

A little while later, my flight time had arrived. Even though I knew exactly what we were about to do, I literally had no idea what to expect. As we taxied towards the runway, I noticed my family watching us from the sideline, I gave them the obligatory thumbs up signal, and off we went. After a few pre flight checks we were trundling down the runway and before I knew it, we came unstuck and began our ascent up to the clouds. In no time at all, we were cruising at two thousand feet towards Headcorn aerodrome. Here cometh the second of my understatements of the highest order. To say I was nervous would be an understatement of the.. well, you get my drift. I was totally incapable of enjoying the fantastic view at my disposal as my heart was pounding, my hands were leaking and for the life of me, I found I couldn't even move.

As I sat there, staring straight ahead, Capt Pittock explained to me that if I were to look outside the plane, across to my left, I would be able to make out the London skyline with its ever-growing cornucopia of recently constructed tall buildings. I don't know about look left, I couldn't move my head if I tried.

As a means of distraction, I focussed on looking at the instruments INSIDE the plane. After about three quarters of an hour, Capt Pittock comfortably delivered me to the sanctuary of the grass runway at Headcorn. We had some lunch at the airfield cafe and as soon as we'd finished our cuppa, we set about our return journey. The strangest thing about all this is the fact that, once we were safely back on the ground, I couldn't wait to get back in the air again. Ten minutes later and we were airborne once more. I was still just as nervous, but this time I managed to look across to the vista of the London skyline, and what a skyline. Fairly soon, we landed back at Biggin Hill where my family members were thrilled to see me arrive back safe and sound, and they could see just how excited I was with the whole experience.

Three weeks later my family accompanied me once again. This time, to my eagerly anticipated 'Loop-de-Loop' flight at Ipswich airport. I was met by the Chief Flying Instructor at Suffolk Aero Club, Debbie. She introduced me to one of her highly experienced instructors who went by the name of Martin. He explained to me the importance for height when doing what we were about to do, and said we would be flying at three and a half thousand feet (the minimum height for aerobatics)

He told me there was no point in worrying too much. He said if anything were to go terribly wrong up there, such as the wings coming off, the fall back down to earth is quite painless. He finished up by saying 'It's only the final inch that hurts.' Thankfully he was grinning like a Cheshire cat when he said that.

So there I was, all prepared (prepared, ha! that's a laugh) for my, 'considerably scarier than the last time I flew in a small plane,' flight. He asked me if I was ready and I replied with the squeakiest response I've ever uttered, 'Yes.' Immediately coughing a couple of times, then repeating my reply, 'Yes,' I said, a little bit louder than I anticipated. I followed him out through the clubhouse door, and we went towards where the planes were parked up. I must have looked a lot like a puppy chasing the ankles of it's human soon after their first meeting.

Martin, slowly, and ever so casually escorted me over the apron where he introduced me to Alpha Foxtrot. AF was a wonderful little Cessna 150 Aerobat. All through the stages of our flight, Martin did his best to make me feel as relaxed as possible. And, to a huge degree, it actually worked.

He ran through everything with me, from the walk around pre-flight checks, with which he followed the strict guidelines of the accompanying check list, the 'into wind' control checks we were about to do, to the unusual angle of attack I would feel as we climbed up to the heavens, and the speed we needed to reach to enable us to take off in the first place. As soon as we were ready for take off, he let me take hold of the control column, push the throttle fully in and, once we had reached 65knots, with a little assistance, and a keen eye on what I was doing, he let me pull back on the yoke and take off.

So, in next to no time we were at a thousand feet, then fifteen hundred feet. We punched through the clouds and within fifteen more minutes, there we were, not at the expected three and a half thousand feet but at four thousand feet, and Martin asked me if I was ready to face the Loop. With my harness firmly holding me in place, I grabbed the straps with both of my hands which by now, were leaking more than ever, and watched as he reduced the throttle and pushed the nose forward to increase the speed. I looked at the Earth, four thousand feet below us. Now, with the perspective of the ground getting ever closer in front of me, I closed my eyes and puffed manically, a bit like, no, a 'LOT' like a woman does when giving birth. As he pulled the nose up into the loop, he increased the throttle to full, and we completed the loop.

The next thing I knew we were straight and level again. Martin asked me if I was ok, to which I replied I was fine. Then he asked me if I wanted to do it again. I didn't hesitate. 'Yes,' I said, as he flew us back up to the desired height. 'Ok,' said he. 'This time, try to keep your eyes open.' Once again, he dipped the nose as I, once again, looked through squinted eyes as the ground came ever closer towards me. He pulled the nose back up and increased the throttle. As we reached the apex I saw the earth had all but disappeared from view, only to see it reappear from the top of the windscreen as we went over the loop. On this occasion, even though I puffed and puffed like billy-oh for a second time, I did manage to keep my eyes open. Wow, what an experience.

After we landed, I asked Martin if he could estimate how many hours I would need to obtain my PPL. He said that, because of my extreme fear of heights, he would estimate it being around the one hundred hour mark. (The bare minimum being forty five hours)

Two weeks later, I was at another airfield. This time, I went to Earls Colne in Essex. I'd booked two lessons there prior to my acrobatic flight at Ipswich. I found the prices there were the most affordable, but because there wasn't that much difference in cost, and even though I had two wonderful flights from Earls Colne, I decided to travel that bit further, and continue with my flight training at Ipswich. Much to my surprise, I was beginning to get quite used to the heights thing. One of the first things I learnt regards flying was, if you want to put someone off from flying with you, or anyone else for that matter, ever again, do some silly unexpected things with them as your passenger.

Simply pushing the controls forward, even just a little bit, can make the most relaxed passenger feel very squeamish when you are a couple of thousand feet up in the air. Thankfully, every instructor I flew with adhered to this mantra, and I treated the same respect to every passenger I took up with me, and there were quite a lot of them over the time.

Because of the distance to the airfield from my place, roughly 90 miles, I used to leave quite early. I'd usually leave my flat about six in the morning. That way, I could get over Tower Bridge before seven o'clock and beat the worst of the traffic. By the time I'd reached Redbridge, most of the vehicles were making their way into London, whereas I was making my way OUT of London. It was a joy the be free of all the cars, vans and lorries. That doesn't mean to say I didn't encounter any traffic on my outbound journey, I did, frequently. But at least it was a lot quieter once on the A12. There were a few occasions where I had the odd lorry right up behind me. But I stuck to my 56mph as that was the best speed for fuel consumption. Plus it was the right speed to get to my destination at the time I'd planned. Some of them got quite bullying, but the closer they got to my car, the slower I drove (within reason) Most of them soon learned to overtake me safely as I would slow down a bit to let them in front once they'd passed me. Having driven the length of the A12 from the M25, right through Essex into Suffolk, I would take a right onto the A14 towards Nacton. But first, I had to cross over the Orwell bridge.

Each and every time I approached it, I made sure to have my tape playing at the same point, Prokovievs 'Romeo and Juliet suite'. The shear size of the bridge never failed to make an impression on me the closer I got to it, and that music seemed to fit the bill perfectly.

Once safely over it, I'd take a left onto the A1189 then take the first exit off the roundabout along the Nacton Road where, after a couple of hundred yards, the entrance to the old Ipswich Airport could be found just on the left hand side.

I always booked two lessons for the day of my visit. One lesson in the morning, then another in the early afternoon. It made no sense to drive all that way, have a lesson then return home, so I always made a day of it. There were many days out throughout that year, and I can honestly say, they were the best days of my life. Sometimes, I could hardly sleep the night before my lessons. When that happened, I would leave my place at two or three in the morning and make my way there.

I'd take a quilt and a pillow with me and, once parked up at the airport, I would get a few hours sleep in the car. Usually, at about 9am, just as the flying school was opening, I'd go in and have a sloosh in the washroom. Then I'd drink a cup, or two, of filtered coffee and I was good to go.

My first lesson was nearly always booked for 10:30, so I had quite a bit of time to prepare myself. The slots were for an hour and a half so after the first flight, I would spend a couple of hours hanging out with whoever was there. I'd watch the other pupils to see how they were progressing and sometimes I'd go up to the control tower to see, and listen, to the other pilots coming and going. Then at 13:30, I would have my second lesson. It never ceased to amaze me, how I could look down at the Orwell bridge and see it getting smaller and smaller the higher I went, but when I drove my car over it, I always had this nervous feeling, knowing how high it was. It was the same with tower blocks. I could never go to the top of a tower block and look over the balcony as I had a serious fear of heights. Even though I knew I wouldn't actually do it, I would visualise myself climbing over the balcony and I'd be hanging on by my fingertips, terrified. Many times in the past, I've ended up, almost collapsing to my knees whenever I had the necessity to call in on someone any higher than the first floor.

But rather strangely, once I got used to flying, I built up a certain tolerance and I could look down at the tower blocks from two, three, even five thousand feet without a problem. It felt as though I was attached to the sky, looking down over a model village.

As I came to the end of my twelfth flying lesson, having done about eleven circuits that day, six in the morning slot and five more that afternoon, all of which entailed landing the plane, taxiing back to the threshold, doing the 'in to wind' power checks and taking off again, I landed the plane once more and taxied back. I faced my little Cessna 150 into wind and just after I completed the usual power checks, my instructor, Ackland, spoke to ATC and informed them of a change of captain, 'The captains name is now Bath,' he said. I couldn't believe it, it was surreal to say the least. He looked at me as he got out and said, 'Just do exactly what you have been doing today and you'll be fine, and be sure to enjoy it.'

So there I was, about to do my first solo. A fete never to be repeated. Sure, you'll fly solo many times after that, but you'll never experience the feeling of that first solo ever again. I contacted ATC and they gave me clearance to take off at my discretion. I checked the T's and P's, made sure the flaps were up, set the trim for take off, pushed the throttle fully in, and away I went.

Bumping along the grass of runway 26, I pressed the right rudder pedal just enough to keep the nose pointing in the direction I wanted to go and as soon as I reached the rotation speed, I gently pulled back on the control column. A couple of more bumps later and she came unstuck. I lowered the nose a touch to build up the airspeed, and as soon as it reached 65kts, I eased the control column back again.

The trim setting made it easy to maintain the right angle of attack and as I got to a height of five hundred feet I started my left turn onto the crosswind leg of the circuit. By the time I'd reached one thousand feet (the circuit height) I turned a little bit more to the left for the downwind leg. I was now flying at a thousand feet, on my own, with no one else with me, just me, all alone, on me own. I squeezed the mic button on the steering yoke and reported my 'downwind' position to ATC. To my left, far below me in the distance, I could see the, almost a mile in length, runway26 serenely passing me by. Then, as I looked straight down, I noticed a school with lots of little dots running around in the grounds.

You've guessed it, those little dots were the kids out on their break, in the playground. Now, with the runway slightly behind me, I turned onto the base leg and let ATC know I was ready to report finals. I reduced the throttle and by the time I had turned onto the final leg of the circuit, I was at the correct height of five hundred feet.

Having reported 'finals' to ATC, I concentrated as best I could on getting myself, and the plane, back down in one piece. With my using the right throttle adjustments, I controlled my rate of descent and, pointing the nose at the runway, I soon found I was nearly there. I looked straight ahead and as soon as the time was right, I flared and gently stuck the plane back on terra firma.

I taxied back to the apron, found my way to the tie down and switched everything off. As soon as I went into the flight school, I was greeted by my instructor and a couple of other students. They could see I was beaming from ear to ear. They even remarked on it as they all, one by one, shook my hand and congratulated me. Only those people that have experienced a first 'solo' flight can ever know quite how it feels. I was dying for a fag afterwards too, but I'd stopped smoking a few weeks earlier.

In fact, it was just after I passed my 'Airlaw' exam (something you must do before you can be sent off on your own) and having passed it, I lit my last cigarette, smoked it, then I said to Acland, 'That's the last time I do that.' True to my word, I've not smoked since. Over the following few months, I flew with Acland, doing all sorts of different exercises from steep turns, stalls and practised forced landings.

I, like many other PPLs, could never understand the need to cram everything into a four week crash course (not the best coin of phrase) as learning to fly is so enjoyable at every stage. Okay, the circuit bashing can get a bit monotonous, and it's where a lot of people tend to drop out and not complete their training. But it does cover the most difficult part of the flying process, that being the LANDING.

I loved every stage of my learning to fly, and it made a lot more sense to stretch the lessons over a longer period of time, and that is exactly what I did. Just over half way through my training, I found myself doing my first cross country flight, with an instructor. Then, not long after that, the time came for me to do my 'solo' cross country flight.

I flew from Ipswich to Peterborough, Connington, landed there and signed in and out. Then I flew from there onto the big airport at Norwich. They have a long, tarmac runway there and lots of heavies (Boing 737s etc) That was quite something, I can tell you. Once again, I signed in and then out and got back into my little Cessna where I took off for my return flight back to Ipswich. All in all, it must have taken two and a half hours of flying time that day.

Over my time at Ipswich, I sat five theory exams, somehow managing to pass them all. Then I took the three practical exams consisting of the cross country flight, the solo cross country flight just mentioned and then last, but by no means least, the GFT (General Flight Test) There is nothing to brag about regards completing the flying training course in forty hours. And there is certainly no shame in completing it in one hundred hours.

It's all good fun and should be enjoyed at every stage, for as long as it takes. In the end, I earned my PPL in about fifty five hours which I believe is average. I took many people up with me over the following few years. Many friends, and even some friends of friends, entrusted me with their lives. Every single one of them said how much they enjoyed it. My mate Phil was my first passenger. I flew him to Stapleford, just on the outskirts of N.E. London.

That was an easy flight as all I needed to do was fly along the A12 until we reached the M25, then turn right and look for the airfield just inside the M25, a couple of miles further on, to our left. After we'd landed, I signed us in and we made our way to the restaurant. I hadn't realised it until we were there, but as we were eating I noticed the road map on the wall (they are a lot different to the flight maps I was now making use of) and I soon found out we were actually in Ongar. It turns out I had just flown us to the very same airfield I'd been taken to by my driving instructor all those years earlier when I was learning to drive. The one where he said I'd never be able to afford to go to.

One day, a couple of years after I qualified, I took one of our members, Joan, to Elstree. Joan and her husband, Tony, owned the C172. We had a bit of lunch there then flew back to Ipswich. One of the best days I had flying, and there were MANY, was when I flew to Ostend and back. I did an ILS landing there. (Instrument Landing System)

Then, once back at Ipswich, Acland told me that one of their instructors, Dave, was flying the C172 the Manchester-Barton airfield to pick up Joan and fetch her back. He asked me if I'd like to go too. He said Dave could do with the company as it was quite a long flight. So, a little while later, off we went to Barton. I flew quite a bit of the way then, as I was starting to feel a bit tired, I gave control back to Dave. Two hours later, we landed at Barton where we met up with Joan in the cafeteria, had a sandwich and a refreshing cup of tea. I sat in the back on the return leg and, not long into the flight, I fell asleep. It seemed quite surreal, dozing at two thousand feet, listening to them both quietly talking about this and that. Then, having fallen into a much deeper sleep, I woke up to see we were just a few miles from our final destination at Ipswich airport.

It's a good thing to note that, flying is not necessarily an activity solely for the rich as, like most of the other people who learn to fly, I sacrificed quite a few things to afford myself the privilege of taking part. I put holidays on hold, even skipping them for a couple of years. I worked a few extra hours and, best of all, I gave up smoking. Once I passed all the exams and flight tests, and became a fully fledged PPL, would you believe, it cost me less per year to keep my pilots license current, than it would have cost me in cigarettes had I still smoked them.

Many times I found myself driving my car to Ipswich with a poorly clutch. Having spent most of my hard earned on the two lessons of the day, I managed to somehow get back home safe and sound, but with a nightshift ahead of me where I earned just enough money to repair the clutch. All that driving meant at least two clutch repairs per year. But it was worth it. Many pilots will tell you, flying is like a drug. Once you get into the habit, it pretty much takes over your life. I can certainly vouch for that.

©Henry James

∾

# YELLOW SUBMARINE/RABBITS

*B*een sitting on the floor in front of my television for the past hour. All peaceful and chilled I was. Enjoying the masterly genius of the psychedelic animations in the animated Beatles film, 'Yellow Submarine'. What with its flashing lights, brilliant colours and weird and wonderful effects, accompanied by some really sublime songs, I thought to myself 'some peoples imaginations are simply amazing, this is blowing me away' then I realised my telly ain't even switched on...

How bizarre!

© John E Bath

~

Rabbits

Aren't people funny. Always hopping around with their big floppy ears flapping about. Tweaking their cute little noses and nibbling at carrots all day. Oh sorry did I say people, I meant Rabbits.

© John E Bath

~

## WISH YOU WERE HERE

*H*i Annabel, you're simply gonna love this photo.

I'll show it to you as soon as I get back from being away from where I was at before I went to this other place which isn't where I'll be when I get back from where I am at the moment.

© John E Bath

~

# HARRY

How can I tell you Harry-cat,
  About the way I feel.
  Remembering when you were happy,
  Remembering how you were ill.
  Yet, now this first year is passing,
  Can my heart withstand this pain.
  And could it be, the sun will return,
  The day we meet again.

Baby boys, baby boys, we miss you now,
  As much as ever, and more.
  Baby boys our love is stronger,
  Yes, our hearts are broken and sore.
  Baby boys we know you had to go,
  Onwards and upwards as they say.
  Yet someday soon, at Rainbow Bridge,
  Someday soon, again we'll play.
  © John E Bath

# MODERN DENTISTRY

*I*sn't modern dentistry marvellous, I have a molar with most of one side missing. Unfortunately, a filling has failed twice.

Rather than fit a whole crown, the dentist suggested I had a 'Half crown' fitted which, fortunately for me, meant I didn't need an injection. So here I am

walking around with Half a Crown in me gob. This pleases me as I much prefer our 'old money' to this decimal stuff.

© John E Bath

What is 'old' money, I hear you ask. Well, if you were born after the UK's coinage system turned decimal, or it's simply been a while since you've thought about pre-decimal coinage, it can be a bit confusing!

On the next page is some rather interesting information. At least, I hope you find it interesting.The advantage of the old system over decimal was that it was easy to divide.

You could divide a pound into:
- Half - 120 pence
- One third - 80 pence
- One quarter - 60 pence
- One fifth - 48 pence
- One sixth 40 pence

In the days before computers and calculators, this was useful for trading.

From the farthing, to the Thrup'nny bit, there's a lot of coins to get your head around. So, here is a guide to the UK's pre-decimal currency!

The Farthing:

1924 George V – 1 Farthing.

The farthing equaled that of a quarter of a penny and it was issued for circulation for nearly 100 years (1860-1956).

This small but significant coin featured the portraits of 11 monarchs, including George I, Queen Victoria, and Queen Elizabeth II.

Half Penny:

1958 QEII Half Penny.

Suggestive of its name, the half penny was worth, literally half of a penny in value. Two farthings would therefore make a half penny!

The last half penny issued for circulation was dated 1967.

Penny:

1922 King George V One Penny.

The pre-decimal One Penny, also known as 1d, held a lot less value than the modern 'New' Penny – there were 240 pennies in a pre-decimal pound!

They were used in circulation from 1714 and the last One Penny was struck in 1967, before the introduction of the 'New' Penny in 1971.

Threepence:

1941 King George VI Threepence.

The 12-sided threepenny (or 3d) is fondly remembered for its individuality. There was quite literally nothing quite like it before, and it holds the proud title of Britain's first non-circular coin since milled coins were introduced in the 17th century.

The unconventional shape and thickness of the new brass Thrup'nny Bit, made it easy to identify amongst other coins in loose change and it quickly proved to be a very popular new addition.

Alongside this brass version of the threepenny, a silver 3d also circulated through the reign of King George V. It even sometimes circulated alongside the brass coin!

Its name derived from It's value, being equal to exactly three pennies.

Sixpence:

1967 Queen Elizabeth II Sixpence.

Also called a 'Tanner' the sixpence was equivalent to one-fortieth of a pound sterling, or half a shilling.

It was first minted in 1551, during the reign of Edward VI, and circulated until 1980.

Throughout centuries, the sixpence has been considered lucky, with fathers slipping one into their daughter's shoe on their wedding day, and families hiding one in their Christmas pudding, in the hope it would bring prosperity and good fortune.

The sixpences continued to be legal tender until 1980 with a value of 2 and a half new pence. The public were so fond of the sixpence, that there was even a 'Save Our Sixpence' campaign!

Shilling:

1938 King George VI One Shilling.

A shilling (or 1/-) was worth 12 pennies and there were 20 in the pre-decimal pound sterling.

The shilling was technically replaced by the five new pence in 1968 in preparation for the decimal changeover in 1971 but they were used as five pence pieces until the 5p was made smaller in 1990.

Florin:

1936 King George V 1 Florin.

The Florin (or Two Shillings, 2/-) was worth 24 pre-decimal pence or two shillings. It was introduced by Victorians in a step towards decimalisation because it was worth one tenth of a pre-decimal pound sterling.

The last Florin intended for circulation was dated 1967 but these coins were used as Ten new pence until the 10p was made smaller in 1990.

Half Crown:

1937 King George VI Half Crown.

The Half Crown (2/6) was worth 30 pre-decimal pence (or two shillings and sixpence). There were eight Half Crowns in a pound sterling.

The last crown for circulation was dated 1967.

Crown:

1965 Elizabeth II (Churchill) 1 Crown.

The English crown was introduced by order of King Henry VIII in 1544 but it wasn't until 1707 that we saw the British crown. It was the successor to the English crown and the Scottish dollar, and it came into being with the Union of Kingdoms of England and Scotland.

It was worth 60 pre-decimal pence or 1/4 of a pound sterling. The legal tender value of the crown remained as 25p until 1990 when their face value was increased to £5 in view of its relatively large size compared to other coins.

With its large size, many of the later coins were primarily commemoratives. The 1965 issue carried the image of Winston Churchill on the reverse, the first time a non-monarch or commoner was ever placed on a British coin, and marked this great mans death.

In 2010, Crowns (£5) were no longer available from banks or post offices and other distributors for face value. They are now reserved for significant anniversaries, birthdays or celebrations and are available to purchase from The Royal Mint and other distributors.

Half Sovereign and Sovereign

1/2 King George V 1/2 Sovereign

Sovereigns had a face value of 20 Shillings (or one pound) and Half Sovereigns of 10 Shillings. As they are made of 22ct Gold, they have a much higher metal value and have not been used as currency in recent years due to this.

Sovereigns are now reserved for flagship royal or historical anniversaries and are only available to purchase from The Royal Mint or official distributors.

~

The pennies were a larger coin than any of the coins we use today. The pound was made of paper like today's £50 note. And we had a paper note for half a pound, which was a ten shilling note. A shilling was often called a "bob"; origins of this nickname are unclear although we do know that its usage dates back to the late 1700s.

Items could also be priced in guineas; a guinea was £1 1s, for instance something could cost 60 guineas, meaning £60 and 60 shillings, or £63. (There was a guinea coin at one time – it was approximately one quarter ounce of gold and was minted in between 1663 and 1814).

Have you ever wondered why an old penny had the sign 'd', rather than a 'p'? It's because it stands for 'denarius', the Latin word for penny (why some countries have still have money called dinars). And the pound sign "£" is an "L" for the Latin word 'libra', which originally meant a pound in weight.

In the classical Roman Empire, standard coinage was established to facilitate business transactions. A pound ('libra') of silver was enough to make 240 denarii. And 12 denarii were worth the same as one gold 'solidus' – so the 's' in £.s.d. really stands for 'solidus' and not for 'shilling' at all!

Meanwhile, the word 'Florin' derives from Florence in Italy, and frequently refers to the 'fiorino d'oro' gold coin struck in that city in 1252. This money format was then borrowed in other countries. In England it was first issued in 1344 by Edward III – at that time it had a value of six shillings, composed of 108 grains (about 7 grams) of gold with a purity of 23 7/8 carats. More recently the name referred to a two-shilling coin.

(All information correct to the best of my knowledge)

# AUNTY VI (SONG)

*A*ny time you're passing by, don't be shy, said Aunty Vi.
Pop in and have a cup of tea.

Any time you're around this way, so many times, I heard her say, call in and pass some time with me.

Cause if you're feeling lonely, and if you're feeling blue.

My door is always open, for you.


So we would put, the world to rights. And talk of all my lonely nights, but she would always perk me up.

When it was time, for me to go, more often than not, she would say no. And just like that, refill my cup.


Then I faced that dreadful day, when she was taken far away, no more would she be there for me.

Thinking of the times we had, and how she made me feel less sad, but maybe I just didn't see;

That she was feeling lonely, and she was feeling blue.

I wish I could have been there,

with my door open too.

Now many years have passed us by, since I drank tea, with
    Aunty Vi, I miss her so, but here's the thing;
    As I sit, and write my songs, I swear she sometimes hums along, and
I can almost hear her sing,
    If you're feeling lonely, if you're feeling blue, my door
    is always open, for you.
    ©John E Bath

# RABBITS

You would think a Rabbit in a hutch, even with the added extra of a small fenced off runaround, would be totally unaware that there is a far bigger world outside of its little bit of space, and you would no doubt be right with that thought.

A Lion or a Tiger born in captivity may know nothing of the outside world either. In fact, any animal born into its restricted, manmade confines, would surely be unaware of the outside world and all it has to offer. Even those animals fortunate enough to be free to live in the wild, still have very limited knowledge of the vastness of the world in which they exist.

We do know that animals exist outside of zoos, in the big wide world. After all, it is us who, rightly or wrongly, incarcerate them in the first place.

That being the case, is it not possible we human beings, restricted to the confines of this planet, know nothing of what's out there in the interminable universe and all it has to offer. Yes, we know it's there, but we know little about it. We believe we know some of what is out there. But what we don't know, far outweighs what we do.

Like a Rabbit in a hutch, with the luxury of a small runaround, are we also confined and denied much of what exists beyond our own boundaries.

A blind man surely, cannot see colours, but they are there, to those with sight. A deaf man may not be able to hear the ensemble of an orchestra, but that too, is there, to those with hearing. I wonder what is out there, that we humans are unable to see, due to our lacking the ability to envisage the bigger picture.

Is it not possible, there is far more out there in and around the billions of galaxies, including our own Milky Way, than we could ever begin to imagine. Could it be that, we ourselves are confined to a type of zoo, and we are being observed by someone, or something, that does have the ability in which to traverse far more of what the universe has to offer. Something that we, no matter how hard we try, and no matter how much we'd like to, will never get to experience.

Someone imprisoned for life, knowing full well that they will live the rest of their days in a small cell, know there is a huge open world with which they can never again freely roam, will eventually become 'Institutionalised'. As time goes on they may well become 'stir crazy'.

Is it not possible, we human beings have very similar ghastly restrictions as a Rabbit in a hutch, a Lion or Tiger in a zoo, a lifer in a cell, thanks to our 'imprisonment' on this planet. Are we somehow being protected from the affliction of going stir crazy by our only being afforded an infinitesimal soupçon of knowledge regards the universe. And with our being undeniably precluded from freely roaming the outer edges of our solar system, and all it has to offer, are we too, compared to someone, or some 'thing' for that matter, institutionalised.

©John E Bath

# MR BOOZE, AND THE MOUSE

I was sitting in my back room listening to my recently purchased Nick Drake CD 'Made to love Magic', the snooker was on telly but was muted as I had no wish to hear the commentary. The French doors were open. It was warm, not quite as hot as was forecast the night before, but was warmish. And then it happened.

Boo da-Booze came in through the open doors with a Mouse in his mouth. It was hanging sideways, all limp and lifeless. Oh, Mr Booze, I thought to my self, (I may have even spoke it out loud but being as I was on my own I have no one to ask, and I'm fairly sure Mr Booze wouldn't remember as he was too fixated with the poor Mouse). 'What am I gonna do with you,' I thought (or said).

I immediately closed the kitchen and living room doors to stop him rushing off and hiding with his new found friend. I quickly managed to take him, still with the poor little mouse hanging from his gob, back out into the garden. He dropped it onto the lawn and as he did so it moved and hopped about a few times, then once again he pounced, wallop.

The poor mouse.

He dropped it for a second time, and as he was towering over the little fella about to go in for the kill, the mouse, just managing to gather the last of his rapidly fading strength, weakly stood upright on his back legs. As he did so he flapped his little hands up towards Mr Booze's face a couple of times. It looked not too dissimilar to a boxer punching one of those small, high level punch balls, but in this case it was as if, well, if you have ever fallen asleep on your chest, then woke up only to find you'd slept on your arms and they have both gone asleep and you can only just about raise them, well, it looked like that. It was so pathetic it was pitiful. It was like he was saying, 'leave me alone you're hurting me'.

Mr Booze was having none of it. Bang, he grabbed the little mouse in his mouth again only this time he had him in his mouth head first. 'Sod it, I'm not allowing this to go on anymore,' I thought, or said (sorry that's enough of that) I grabbed hold of Mr Booze and, even though he struggled like a demented chimp, it wasn't long before he dropped Mr mouse back down onto the grass again.

Looking dishevelled and rather dazed, it soon became apparent that Mr mouse wasn't too badly hurt. A bit shaken after his ordeal but well enough to hop off over the lawn and into the shrubs and trees. The poor little thing, I felt so sorry for it.

I carried the demented chimp, er, I mean, Mr Booze, back inside and closed the doors. His heart was thumping like mad, and even though he was going mental for a while, he soon settled down.

A couple of hours later he was doing almost the same thing once again, only this time with an eight foot tall spider. Well it was big anyway. Sorry to have to report, I didn't manage to save the spider.

©John E Bath

❧

118

# MY DREAM

*W*ow, I mean, WOW. What a dream.

I woke up this morning having dreamed all the houses in my little street in Fulham had been demolished and mostly grassed over. I was in now in my sixties, most of my hair had gone and I had very few remaining teeth, and they were in a dismally poor condition to say the least. Elvis was dead, and there were only two Beatles left and they, along with Mick Jagger, Ray Davis and Cliff Richard were nearly 80 years old. It makes me wonder if 1968 is gonna turn into a bit of a nightmare. Phew.

©Jeremy Nash

# MY FIRST PINT

$\mathcal{I}$ was recently asked the questions:
'When was the first time I got served in a pub, how old was I at the time and how much did the drink cost?'

Just a few seconds later, I recalled the time I bought my first pint. It was a pint of cider, and it was in a pub in Seaton, South Devon, followed by one or two or three more, throughout that memorable night out. My mate Ian and I were holidaying there in the summer of 1974. We, well me anyway, must have looked about 12 years old. I was actually 16 and the Rubettes were at number one in the pop charts with 'Sugar Baby Love'.

The pub staff must have known we were underage but at the same time they probably knew we were on holiday, so we were served without a hitch. Too much time has passed for me to remember the name of the pub, or how much the drinks costs back then, but I do believe we got a little bit tiddly that night.

We've all been there. Met someone we really liked, fell in love, said you'll write and promise to visit soon. Well I was no exception. Tina was her name. She came from a little place called Oswaldtwistle, near Accrington in Lancashire.

She was with a few other 5th form lads and lasses from their school (I was still at school too at the time, seeing as you asked) I can still hear them singing the name of their town 'O.S.W.A.L.D—T.W.I.S.T.L.E' in their broad Lancastrian accents.

And I Ian went on a couple of excursions with them that week. One day we went to the zoo and on another occasion we went to the coast at Paignton. Me and Tina walked along the pier, we bought some candy floss, a couple of Kiss-me-Quick hats and I bought us a couple of nice rings from the gift shop there.

We popped into a record shop where Tina bought me the Rubettes album, 'Wear It's At'. Can you believe it, I still have that LP and listen to it on the odd, but increasingly rare, occasion. Having said that, there is one particular track titled 'Your Love,' that still stands the test of time today. It's such a shame it never gets played on the radio as it's a really beautiful song. I asked the man behind the counter if they had anything by 'The Doors,' to which he replied, 'Yes sir, a fire extinguisher and a bucket of sand.'

Then, in the blink of an eye, the holiday came to an end, and it was all over. A week after I returned home, I got a Dear John letter from her, and yes, you've guessed it, I still have it here somewhere. Many years afterwards, in the June of 1987, I was working for a heating company based in Kings Cross. They supplied us engineers with a van which we were permitted to take home after work. The time came where I was due a weeks holiday so I asked if I could use the van while on leave to visit Brighton for the day.

They were kind enough to allow me to do this, but me being me, I was never known for doing things by halves, I went on a road-trip and drove up to Yorkshire where I stayed in a pub in Arkengarthdale for the night. Then, the next day, after I had a drink in the Tan Hill Inn (Britains highest elevated pub) I dared to venture a bit further north to Scotland. Once there, I booked into a hotel that I'd actually sat outside in dads van when I was about 11. Mum, dad, my sister and I spent a week by the banks of Lock Ken in our parents Bedford Dormobile in the early 1970s and, being as kids were not allowed inside pubs back then, me and my sister had our obligatory bottle of coke and some crisps while we waited in the van.

The next day I set about travelling south, all the way down to north Devon, Lynton and Lynmouth to be precise. As I was motoring it down the M6 making my way there, I noticed the road signs for Preston, then Blackburn.

That's where Accrington is,' I thought.

That's where Oswaldtwistle is; and how close am I?' I thought.

For some unknown reason I've never forgotten her address.

Shall I pop in to see her?

Should I not?

If I met her, would I feel a bit foolish?

Would she still be there? Would I get embarrassed? Would SHE get embarrassed?

There was only one way to find out..........

A couple of hours later, having bumbled my way into Oswaldtwistle, I met several wonderful people at the roadside with the most fantastic Lancashire accents. Eventually, I found someone that knew exactly how I could find the street I was looking for. A little while after that, having followed their directions (I had no map) there I was, parked up outside the house I'd been seeking. Full of trepidation, I gazed at the front door and nearly bottled it, but something made me switch off my engine. I noticed a young man washing his car on the drive. Nervously, I got out of my van and approached him. 'Excuse me mate, sorry to trouble you but does a Tina Cxxxxxn live here at all?'

As it happens, he turned out to be Tina's brother and, even though she herself had moved out of the family home several years earlier, she was actually indoors visiting her mum that very minute.

Her brother, with the best Paddy McGuiness accent ever, called to her through the open front door. 'Tina,' he said. 'There's a chap out here wants a word with you.' A couple of seconds later, Tina popped her head out of the door, as did her mum behind her. She looked at me quizzically, as if she didn't even know me. Of course, she didn't know me. Many years had gone by, and a lot of water had passed under the bridge since that holiday; I introduced myself.

'Hello Tina,' said I. Then, after a short pause, I said 'Seaton, Devon.'

She said, 'That were thirteen odd years ago.' Then she looked at me and said, with a somewhat bemused and surprised look appearing on her face, 'John?'

'Yes,' said I (feeling quite relieved she didn't ask me if I was Ian)

'Do you want a brew?' she asked.

So, in I popped, and we had a bit of a catch up, and a brew or two. Or was it three? She told me she was now married, with two kids.

It turned out, as luck would have it, she was visiting her mum while waiting for the kids to come back from school. One of which, came in while I was there. I was so glad I mustered up the courage to pay her a visit and we both had a blast talking about this and that.

All too soon, the time came for me to say my good-byes, and continue with my road trip. As I was leaving, Tina got her brother to take a couple of photos of us by my van, for prosperity. A short time later, I was back on the M6 making my way to Devon. A few hours after that, I arrived. I found a lovely little B & B to stay at, and freshened up.

I had a bit of a snack, then went out to have a couple of pints while I reminisced about that afternoons adventure. To say I felt a bit sad after my unplanned Oswaldtwistle visit, would be an understatement. I put that down to my having had to leave her and set off on my own, for a second time in my short life. The next day, I decided I couldn't bare to be alone any longer, so I cancelled the rest of my road-trip and drove, some-what hurriedly, back to Fulham where I met up with my mum and dad down the 'Sajacs' (a social club, long since gone) I have to say, that night, I got quite, quite drunk.

It took a few days, but the 'recently opened old wounds' of sadness soon began to heal, and I was back on track, with the rest of my life ahead of me. I'm so glad I was brave enough to call in on Tina. I'm more than certain I made the right decision. As for the three questions I'd originally been asked, well, managing to answer one out of the three can't be too bad.

©John E Bath

~

# GROWING PAINS

*S*he was smiling as she stood there. She was saying something, but I couldn't hear what was said. It didn't matter though. She was there, smiling as she spoke, and I was smiling too.

I felt happy again, as she stood there.

But she didn't move. It was as if time had stood still.

It didn't matter though.

She was there, smiling as she stood, and I was smiling too.

Then just like that, she wasn't there anymore.

All I had was the Rubettes LP we'd bought, from the little shop, by the pier, a few weeks earlier. Plus the obligatory Dear John letter of course. Then, my heart sank as I awoke, as she, just like my smile, had gone.

Now, many years have passed, since that week we spent together. But the memory of it, still remains today.

And I always regain my smile, when I take the time to listen while, my Rubettes songs, once more, begin to play.

© John E Bath

# ART

*I* think the marriage of subtle tones, along with the abstract, paradox extremities, blend well with the autonomous colours whilst not distracting from the images vision of giving it an almost ambiguous personification of impetuousness. This, in my most humble of opinions, truly implements the realisation that ones existence is mortal. Other than that, it's a bit shit.

©John E Bath

# THE PHOTO

*I*ncluded here is the letter I sent to my friend, Ken McCormack on the 13th August 2018 at 20:30pm. I first met Ken back in the Autumn of 2001. We were outpatients attending a day hospital for people with severe depression. After the completion of our time there, several of us, including Ken, stayed in contact, but by the end of 2005, Ken went off grid, and we lost touch for about three years.

Then one day, completely by chance, I spotted him in the High Street. I followed him into a Farm Foods shop and surprised him. We remained good friends after that and, with the help of modern day social media, we managed to regularly stay in contact. A few of us continued to meet up and watch the odd band here and there, and we always made sure to invite Ken along. He really enjoyed those nights, and we could see he was always happy to join us. Then the day came where he told us of his illness. It was the worst news ever. It meant he had limited time left, but he remained strong, a lot stronger than I could ever be. Over the following few months, he shared lots of photos of his time with his family. He kept us all up to date with how he was coping mentally and even shared some photos of his nights out with us. With the fantastic support of his family, he even managed to visit his favourite place, Glastonbury Tor.

There was one particular photo he shared from that day that caught my eye. It was of him and his son. They both stood there smiling bravely at the top of the Tor.

As I looked at the photo, I noticed his yellow boots. He did like yellow boots, did Ken. Later that day, I started to write a poem about the very first time I met him, about how he had struggled and of course, his yellow boots.

Here is that actual letter, followed with the poem.

'Hi mate, I'm sorry I've not written to you sooner. I don't think I've ever told you this but, back in the days when we attended Chiltern Day Hospital, my first memory of you was your wonderful yellow boots. I noticed them as you entered the room where the large group meeting was taking place.

Because I was feeling quite poorly at the time, I was just staring at the floor feeling lost. All I could see was this pair of yellow boots as you sat opposite me in the circle of chairs. That's the everlasting memory I have of my first day there. Some time later, once I'd started to improve, I went and bought myself my very own pair of yellow boots.

I'm sure you have had several pairs since then but I did notice, in the photo you recently shared on Facebook, you were wearing another pair this past weekend during your visit to Glastonbury Tor. Yesterday, this poem came to mind so I started to write it down. Today I polished it up a bit. I've dedicated it to you my friend. I sincerely hope it doesn't cause you any upset as that is the last thing I want to do. I hope you like it. I've titled it 'The Photo', and it goes like this.'

## The Photo

When I saw those yellow boots, upon the Glastonbury Tor.
    It broke my fragile heart, I might not see them anymore.
    The first time that I saw them, I was staring at the floor.
    We'd all sat in a circle, as you came in through the door.


You quietly made your entrance, and you quietly sat in your chair.
    And it was after you quietly spoke, I noticed you were there.
    The kindest man imaginable, who's life had turned so cold.
    The kind of man so gentle, once born, they broke the mould.


You've got through so much in your life, you always fought and
    won. I hope that there is so much more, for you that can be done.
    Be strong my friend, as I know you are. Be strong, and stand your
    ground. The world is a far richer place, in having you around.


When I see those yellow boots, upon the Glastonbury Tor.
    My heart gets filled with hope, that I will get to see them, more.
    When I see those yellow boots, as the years have passed us by.
    I know many pairs have come and gone, and I try so, not to cry.


So I've printed out the photo, and I put it in a frame.
    I know they're not your first pair, but I like them all the same.
    Now I've hung the photo in my hall, and I really have to say.
    I'm happy in the knowledge, that I will see them every day.

Then if people ask me why it is, I have that photo on my wall. I'll tell them it reminds me, of the kindest man of all.

And as I check the photo of those boots, each time I go out my door. I remind myself, that someday soon, someday soon, I'll visit the Tor.

©John E Bath


I'm so very pleased to be able to report that my friend Ken got straight back to me to say he was delighted with the poem. Sadly, just a few short months later, on the 27th September, Ken died.

After the service had finished, upon leaving the chapel, I learnt I wasn't the only one to have noticed his boots as, outside amongst the floral tributes for all to see, someone had placed a beautiful pair of yellow boots with flowers in them. How lovely was that.

A little while later, having read all the tributes, we arrived back at the hall. There was plenty of 'Ken' memorabilia dotted about here and there. As we were drinking tea etc, I was escorted to one particular table where I was shown the poem I'd written. It had been placed there by one of his family members. What an honour.

R.I.P. Mate.

# DON (SONG)

 There's a girl, in my life, and I love her.

But she can't be my wife, but I love her.

Of all the other girls I've known, they've always left me feeling sad and blue, and oh so lonely. Now I know, she's the only, one for me. I'm happy to say, she's gonna live with me anyway.

And this girl, in my life, she loves me.

She can't be my wife, but she loves me.

She's never known any other man.

I am the only one, she's ever loved, and she seems

happy. Even though, she's sometimes snappy.

She loves to see me, everyday, and these are the things that

she likes to say, she says;

Meow, meow meow, meow meow, meow meow.

Meow meow meow, meow meow meow.

(Yeh, I know, she's a girl, her name was Don…. It's a long story)

©John E Bath

# GROANS THREE

What did the left eye say to the right eye? Between you and me, something smells.

~

I went to buy a goldfish last week. The bloke asked me if I wanted an aquarium. I said, I couldn't give a monkies what star sign it is.

~

When the time comes, I want to die peacefully in my sleep, just like my grandfather did. Not screaming in terror like his passengers.

~

Two wind turbines side by side on a wind farm. One says, 'I really like jazz music.' The other one says, 'I'm a heavy metal fan.'

~

I was playing chess with my mate when he said, 'Let's make this interesting.' So we stopped playing chess.

A bloke started to tell a girl a 'dumb blonde' joke in his local pub when the girl, who was herself blonde, stopped him in his tracks. 'Excuse me,' she said. 'Before you continue, I think it's best you are aware that I'm a blonde, my friend and my four sisters sitting over there are all blondes. Are you sure to want to carry on with your silly joke?'

He slowly looked at her, thought for a few seconds and said, 'Nah, not if I'm gonna have to explain it six times.'

# NORMAN WISDOM

Not many people had us laughing,
    Out loud so much it caused pain.
Running around like a demented child,
Madcap comedy, again and again.
Always a clown but with a heart of gold,
No one else, has ever come near.
With a smile, a song and an infectious laugh,
In seconds you`d have us in tears.
Singing a song, you once asked of us,
Don`t laugh at me cause I`m a fool.
One things for sure, Norman, me old mate,
Most of us never thought that at all.
© John E Bath

# DAD

My dad, he wears a deaf aid, but he never turns it on.
When he does, he never hears you, cos the battery's always gone. He sits
back, in the corner, away from all the crowd. When our family get
together, they're always very loud.

He likes to do his garden, planting flowers, and all his veg. But he has to
wear a woollen hat, cos the cold gets to his head. He's a flashy little
fellow. And a jolly little gent. Although he's 75 years old, his bones are
straight, not bent.

He's a bingo caller down his club, shouting all the numbers out. As soon
as everyone's gone home, he nips off, for his pint of stout. He has helped
his children, one by one. He has treated them all the same. So, if they did
do something wrong, our dad was not to blame.
So dad, from all your children, thanks for what you have done. You
made life very good for us. And we're glad you married mum.
©Muriel Buckingham (nee' Hatchett)

## MY FRIEND THE SPARROW

My friend the Sparrow, just flew in to say, 'Hello Mr. human, how are you today? I like your patio, I like your grass, I like the way it tickles my.... feathers.

I like your plant pots, your flowers and your seeds, I also like.......er, your abundance of weeds. I like your pond from which I can drink, I like your pond in which I can think.

I like your greenhouse, and orangery too.
And your mosaic hot tub, of red, white and blue.
Your summerhouse is cosy, on warm humid nights,
where I can survey your most exquisite, gardenery delights.
Your swimming pools are heated and are warm throughout the day,
and when the sun is out of sight, they still remain that way.
For oft` I see your famous friends, indulging in the waters.
Where Lisa Marie is regularly seen, playing with Obama's daughters.
But wait, you place is tiny, with a totally different view.
And where's the pools and summerhouse, and hot tub of red, white and blue.

The Orangery's gone, the greenhouse has gone, and so have the famous and rich. I guess that's why I'm glad I'm a Sparrow, for you sometimes life is a bitch.


A little bird once told me, once a little bird like me,

learns to fly and spread his wings, and sets off to be free.

He'll meet all sorts of lifeforms, from the nice to the really quite bad. And he'll dream of dreams of humans, those of wealth, some with nothing, some sad.

But when he hears of someone who's really good, to the creatures great, and small. Fly in with a chirp, and say a cheery hello, and have yourself a ball. For they'll give you seed and all sorts of food, for you to enjoy as you wish. But try not to make them angry, like the Heron, who eats their fish.'

©John E Bath


('The word had got around of 'Mr Booze', tormenting that poor little mouse. And how I released it on to the lawn, then kept 'him' in the house. I guess that's the reason Mr. Sparrow, dropped in to say 'how are you?' For should he find he has trouble, he knows I'll help him too.')

# WALK-IN WARDROBE

'I think I'll carry on doing some more work to my walk-in wardrobe,' I thought.

'It's really quite good,' I thought.

It has lots of hanging rails with coats, shirts and jeans etc. There aren't any doors to cover them, but that's cool. It has lots of boxes on the floor for storage, and it's got lots of shoes scattered about all over the floor. It's got a bed in it in which to sleep and, oh, hang on a minute, it's my bleeding bedroom. God, it's so untidy. What WAS I thinking?

©John E Bath

# THAT DOGS FACE

*T*hat dogs face looks sad to me,
    Hairy, with large, tired eyes.
All the other dogs pick on him,
That dogs face tells no lies.


Daily struggles are all too real,
    Over time, his health will pay.
    Going home is never a choice,
    So that dog lives as a stray.


Feeling lost in this great big world,
    Alone with no one to chase.
    Children feed him now and again,
    Everyone knows that dogs face.
© John E Bath

# THE WAY YOU'RE ALWAYS TURNING DOWN THE SOUND, OF MY TOM WAITS SONGS (SONG)

The way that you caress my hand, makes me feel so warm from deep inside,
that my feelings I can't hide, because I love you so.
And when you look me in the eyes, it's then I realise that you're for me, but I just can't make you see, how much I love you so; cause,

You're full of shit, you think you're really it, but you'll end up on the shelf,
just like my uncle Elf said, these things ain't meant to be, for the likes of you and me……..
You only see, just what you want to see. You're never gonna be,
any good to anyone else, you only ever think of yourself, and one day you'll be old and lonely.

Nobody told me, about the lies you tell.
And nobody told me, you was an 'orrible girl.
But my Muvva warned me, yes,
my Muvva warned me. My Muvva marked me
cards about you and your sort.

So you think I've got an evil mind, well I'll tell you girl; I'm not as blind as you. I've seen the things you do. You just leave men feeling blue and lonely.

And the way that you keep banging on, makes me want to pack my things and go;

cause you just don't wanna know when I say how I love you.


But you're full of shit, you think you're really it, you'll end up on the shelf,

just like my uncle Elf said, these things ain't meant to be, for the likes of you

and me

I'm going for a beer, and then I'll have a drink or two on you and when I get back

I don't want you to be here. Get out of my face, you're a disgrace;

The way you wag your tongue, it's like a ringing in my ears, it's been going on for

years, and I just can't take no more, there's the door

Leave me alone.

I'll live on my own,

Scarred for life.

The way you wag your tongue.

The way you sleep around.

The way you're always turning down

the sound, of my Tom Waits songs;

Leave me alone…………………….

© John E Bath

∽

# SIXTY

*a*m I really nearly sixty, have my fifties almost passed.
    I knew my twenties would pass me quick, and my
thirties wouldn't last.
But my forties went in the blink of an eye, and I feel it's just not fair.
Thinking of my teeth, I love them both, but I really miss my hair.


I know I won't be on my own, my mates are ageing too.
    Some are quite gummy, and some are bald,
    and, like mine, their decades flew.


Some got married, some stayed alone.
    Some loved and lost and cried.
    Some married again and are still together.
    Unfortunately some have died.
    Am I sad I'm getting older ?
    Going mutton, with a creaky old voice.
    No I'm not, I'm alive and kicking.
    So many, denied that choice.

So, when I see my mates on Facebook,
    as they share their photos from their phone.
    I'm happy to see their ageing too,
    and it's not just me, on my own.
    © John E Bath

# CAN A POET DRY THE TEARS

*D*o poets cry the tears, of a thousand broken hearts,
      as they pen the words we're all compelled to read.
Do painters paint the sight, of a hundred million eyes,
as they feed the hunger of our abstract need.


Do sculptors sculpt the shape, of a hundred marble souls,
      as they chip away at all our darkest fears.
Do singers kiss the words, as they echo from the stage,
then caress the admiration of their peers.


Can a painter or a sculptor tend the wounds of mother Earth?
      Or a singer halt the onslaught of ones greed.
Can a poet dry the tears, of a thousand broken hearts,
as a million broken more, begin to bleed?
© John E Bath

# HISTORY OF FULHAM GAS WORKS

*A*s children, my sisters and I attended many a wonderful xmas party at Fulham Gas Works. Our father worked for the gas board from the 1950s onwards, and they put on some really good do's. We were often quite spoilt regard the spread, being treated to an assortment of cakes, jelly, soft drinks and all sorts of entertainment. The clown did a great turn, and even Father Christmas made an appearance and called us up to the stage, one by one, to give us a present (with the added bonus of an orange and a bit of chocolate in a paper bag).

In the evening, we were taken by coach to Wembley Arena and other such venues, where we would watch a Christmas show such as Snow White on Ice, Cinderella on Ice etc. I think the grown-ups had a blast too, probably down the pub. There were several other employee activities that occurred throughout the year. The gas board even had their own sports ground in Acton, where many a football tournament regularly took place. They also held lots of Discos in the hall at the sports ground. Once I'd reached the age of 15, my sisters (who are a teeny, weeny bit older them me) and a few of their girl friends, took my cousin Charlie and I along with them to a few of the Xmas and New Year parties held there.

Upstairs to the offices in the gasworks, where the kids parties I went to were held, were three full sized snooker tables. When I was 12, my dad and his friend took me with them to see if I would like to play. No one knew at the time, not even my school, but I was really short sighted. There was no way I could pot a ball on a table that size, it was far too blurry. Plus, to be fair, I couldn't hold a cue to save my life. Not that many years later, I played on those same tables dozens of times as it became my place of work (plus I wore glasses)

By then, I was doing my apprenticeship with NTGB. We'd moved there from the smaller depot which was utilised for years in Pulton Place, just opposite Fulham Police Station (Now, unbelievably, long gone) We had a nice little canteen at the Pulton Place depot. Peggy was the woman that worked in the canteen. She was lovely. She always served up a great cuppa, did Peggy. Plus she cooked up some real nice dinners, many of which I thoroughly enjoyed back in the day.

Sadly, there wasn't a place for her at the new gas depot, so I never saw her after that. That's not entirely true as, many years later, shortly after my old mum went into Wentworth Court residential housing on the Bayonne Road estate, I was in the main reception area, talking with the warden, Phyllis. As she was helping me with my enquiry, I couldn't help but notice an elderly lady sitting on her own, waiting to be attended to. Apparently it was her first day there. She looked a bit lost, but I knew her straight away so, as Phyllis was checking my mums files, I asked the lady if she was called Peggy. Sure enough, it was the lady from the canteen all those years earlier. I told her who I was and how we would have known each other. It was so nice to see her, albeit, at a much later stage of her life. And, even though she couldn't recall me, I like to think she felt a little bit more familiar with her new surroundings after that.

One of the older fitters I worked with, Charlie Ridge, was a top snooker player. He won quite a few tournaments for the gas board team did Charlie. There were several other older fitters that I worked with throughout my apprenticeship. I remember seeing a few of them when they reached retirement age. With tears in their eyes, they always looked a bit dazed as they were presented with a clock and a golden handshake.

Having started as apprentices as soon as they left school at age fourteen, it was as if they were wondering where all the years had gone. Now, here I am at very close to that same retirement age, and I too wonder where the years have gone. Back then, I selfishly wanted to work with the younger fitters as they tended to let you have more 'hands on' experience, plus they took you to the pub most afternoons when we finished early. With the older ones, you usually ended up sitting in the van at a quarter to five where they would look at you, give you a cheeky wink, and say ' Go on, you can shoot off now if you like, as if they were doing you a big favour.'

If only they knew. One of the old guys, a man by the name of Cyril, was very meticulous in his work. All the fitters were careful with their jobs, but the older ones like Cyril took it to another level. My dad told me it was because they were wiser, and far more experienced, and they would have learned many lessons with some of the awful things they had seen over their time. After all, working with gas entails a great deal of responsibility, and it was their attentiveness that kept them, and their customers, safe.

I remember sitting in the little two tone grey mini van with Cyril on several occasions. He would bore me senseless with his wartime stories. I was only eighteen at the time and I was used to going to the pub, having a couple of beers and playing pool. These days, I would find it an absolute privilege to have the honour to be in his company and listen to his life experiences and war stories. I'd buy him drinks all night long for the honour. I have so much respect for him and his generation. I don't doubt for one minute he would be one of the most interesting of people to spend time with. I'd give anything to be able to listen to what he had to say now. Alas, that can never be.

Recently, while researching some local history, I was most saddened to learn of an awful incident that was to befall Cyril and his family. It happened about ten years before I started on the gas board. I never once heard talk of it when I was working there. I wonder if any of the other fitters or supervisors knew of it. The poor man. For the sake of respect to his family, and to uphold some privacy, I'll say no more on that matter.

~

Now for some historical information regards the gasworks itself:

Mr. C. J. Fret, the accomplished author of 'Fulham Old and New,' points out that on 28th June 1383 Warenus de Insula, or Warren de Lisle, died in possession of a house at Fulham which he held of John Saundford, and this was in all probability Sandford Manor House. He was a man of mark, and in 1367 his daughter Margaret had married Thomas, the fifth Earl of Berkeley, who succeeded to the estate at Sands End. After that it passed, also by marriage, to Richard Beauchamp, the Earl of Warwick, who at his death in 1439, owned land in half the counties of England, including in Fulham 'The Lord Lyle's Place.'

Shortly afterwards it seems to have come into the hands of the Collegiate Church of St. Martin. Indeed, according to a statement by Lysons, which does not agree with the account given above, Henry, the Earl of Northumberland presented it to that foundation as early as the year 1403. In any case, it is an undoubted fact that king Henry VIII, having granted that church with all its endowments to Westminster Abbey at the Dissolution, Sandford Manor passed into the hands of the Dean and Chapter of Westminster, who, in 1549, handed it over to Edward VI in exchange for land elsewhere. In 1558 it was sold by Queen Mary to William Maynard, citizen and mercer of London, when it consisted of 11 acres of meadow and 43 acres of arable land. In 1630 Sir William Maynard, his son, died in Ireland, being then possessed of the property.

A halo of romance is gathered round Sandford Manor House because of Nell Gwynne's supposed connection with it. We have even been told that it was built for her by Charles II, although the style of the house is undoubtedly earlier, and we know that it continued to belong to the Maynards till the latter half of the 18th century. In the 'Gentleman's' magazine for March of the present year, there is a pleasant article in which will be found all that can be said in favour of this tradition. The writer seems convinced that the popular actress here found a home, that 'the rooms rang with much of her laughter,' and that in the quiet garden 'her good angel came to her and taught her how to work towards assisting in the comfort of the poor and afflicted.'

Indeed, Faulkner, the historian of Fulham and Chelsea, who, writing in 1812, says positively that 'the fair Eleanor' resided at Sandford Manor House, his chief piece of evidence being that a medallion in plaster of her had some years previously been found on the estate, and was then in possession of the owner. Other relics were also discovered, including a thimble with the initials N.G. engraved upon it. I doubt very much it was Noel Gallagher, sir Nigel Gresley or Noel Gordon (Crossroads) and, as Mr. Fret tells us, 'an alleged Freemason's badge or jewel supposed to have belonged to Charles II was found in a secret compartment under the boards of a room on the first floor.' It was presented by the then occupant, Mr. McMinn, to his Lodge. Four walnut trees formerly in the garden were said to have been planted by 'royal hands,' while, according to another tale of old, our 'Charlie Boy' himself, once rode his horse or pony up the, by no means spacious, staircase (Twat)

The *Domestic Intelligence* for August 5, 1679, contains the following information:

'We hear that Madame Ellen Gwynne's mother, sitting lately by the water side at her house by the neat houses near Chelsey, fell accidentally into the water and was drowned.' Mr. Fret suggests that this accident may have happened here, and not on the low ground near the Thames side at Pimlico, as is generally supposed. A large pub near the Manor House was for many years titled the 'Nell Gwynne' and her memory was cherished in the neighbourhood. But, since the 1980s it has undergone several different name changes, From The Ink Bar, with its sister watering hole that went by the name of The Pen in Parsons Green Lane; (Pen and Ink, geddit?) The Jam Tree; One; Come the Revolution and the latest which I've seen is rather bafflingly, named The Lost Hours.'

You may well ask, why am I submitting all this information about Sandford Manor House? Well, I'll tell you. Are you sitting comfortably? Great, then I shall begin. My old workplace, Fulham Gas Works, was actually built on the site of Sandford Manor by the Imperial Gas Light and Coke Company which started construction of its works 1824. A certain Mr Samuel Clegg being its first engineer.

Gas works were used to produce and store flammable coal gas. Coal was mined in Britain, and then shipped on a barge up rivers or on trains to the gas works. There it was burned to create the gas, which was then purified and put into the gas holders until it was needed to light streets and buildings. In 1829 it commenced the manufacture of gas.

In 1876 ( the year of my paternal great grandfather, John's birth) the Imperial was absorbed by the Gas Light and Coke Company. A Carburetted Water Gas plant was added much later in 1899. Its ornately decorated number two gasholder is Georgian, and was completed in 1830. It is reputed to be the oldest gasholder in the World. In 1949, when the gas industry was nationalised, the North Thames Gas Board became the responsible authority.

From 1908 to 1917, low gravity gas was made in a separate plant and distributed to the Hurlingham Club for use in Balloons, both for leisure and war activity. In 1911, the Gas Light and Coke Company built its first workshop and transport depot at Fulham, adding a mantle burning off factory in 1916, and a Benzole motor spirit loading station (petrol pump to you and me) was added in 1920. In 1927 a new Research Laboratory was built which was extended in 1942 and 1955. The works was connected to the Kensington Canal which was used to transport coal to the plant. From 1926 the coal arrived at a riverside wharf from sea going colliers.

An Act of Parliament was passed in 1859, to build the West London Extension Railway (WLER) which was to connect with the West London Railway line from Willesden to Kensington and cross the river Thames to Battersea. Provision was made in the 1859 Act for the WLER to lay a siding into the gas works. However, having been abandoned in 1861, the connection was actually made a tad later and the WLER commenced operations in 1863. Consisting of about thirty acres with a large river frontage, it wasn't until 1926 that the Gas Light and Coke Company built a wharf which enabled sea-faring colliers to deliver their loads without needing to transfer it to barges capable of entering the docks. They had two shunting locomotives and, in keeping with the King Charles II theme, one of the locos was named the Nell Gwynne (Unfortunately it was totally destroyed during a wartime bombing raid on the 18th of September 1940) and the second one was named the Charles II.

The ill fated Nell Gwynn was replaced by an Andrew Barclay 0-4-0 saddle tank. The GLCC also had their own rolling stock consisting of many wagons. There was always quite a few of them to be seen mingling with the fleet of road transport vehicles, as well as those in the works sidings. The Charles II was eventually sold off and went to Messrs TW Ward of Grays. The Andrew barclay saddle tank went to West Thurruck where is was furnished with the name 'Planet.'

With the advent of North Sea gas in the 1970s, the gasworks closed down and several car breakers yards later occupied much of the site. An old mate of mine from the 1990s, Tony, had one. I loved looking around the yard and checking out all those old motors, I mean, who doesn't 8-) It was a thriving industry in its day, from the time of construction right up to the end of the 1970s/early 1980s. Now, the gas works, just like the rest of the land once owned by GLCC, all along Imperial Road and Town-mead Road, has all but disappeared. It has all been redeveloped mostly, and quite insanely, for accommodation. Now, the land once occupied by the original Watson House and Malcolm House in Townmead Road, even the old transport depot, is flats. The other Watson House, in Peter-borough Road, now consists of multi-million pound 'Loft style' apartments.

The works was always known for its innovative design and methods, and for a while had the largest holders in existence.. The Imperial Gasworks neoclassical office building (my old office) was completed in 1857. This office building can be regularly seen at the start of the 1970s tv series, 'The Sweeney,' as Regan (John Thaw) is seen running past the entrance at the start of the program. Many episodes were filmed in and around Fulham, including the back of the gasworks. In 1927, a laboratory designed by the architect Sir Walter Tapper was added. All three struc-tures are now Grade II listed buildings. Not that that affords them 100% security against developers but, for now at least, they are relatively safe.

~

# A BRIEF INSIGHT OF BAYONNE ROAD

*Number 48 Bayonne Road is the first house to the right of this corner shop*

Bayonne Road was much like any other road in this part of Fulham. Having been successfully utilised as farmland for many years, it undertook a huge change in the late 19th century. Many rows of terraced houses went up and by the end of the 1800s a large community was developing.

My maternal grandparents lived at number 8 Bayonne Road. They raised my mum and her brothers and sisters there. As a lad growing up, I had some really good neighbours. There were always plenty of other similar aged kids to play with back then.

I was actually born in the front room of number 48 Bayonne Road back in the late 1950s. I had several cousins living there too, as my mums sister Kate married and brought her children up above the tyre shop on the corner of Bayonne Road and Greyhound Road. Another of my mums sisters, Violet, raised her family at number 10 Bayonne Road, and my mums sister Patricia married Fred White, of 19 Bayonne Road, and they also lived there for a while. One of mums brothers, Jim brought his children up at number 42 Bayonne Road.

Having recently been doing some research of the street that I grew up in, I found some rather tragic information from the British Newspaper Archive website regards some unfortunate occurrences that happened in my old street in the past.

As well as a murder attempt upon a wife by the husband in 1902, there were at least two tragic child deaths, one in 1904 and the other in 1924. In 1907, a seventeen year old lad was charged with attempted murder after he fired three shots at his girlfriend, one of which hit her (both of them came from Bayonne Road but lived at separate addresses) A young lad was sent to Borstal in 1950, there were several middle aged deaths. In 1939, a 53 year old widows death was accelerated by her own neglect as she wouldn't see a doctor. A man was killed in an accident at his place of work in 1936. There was a case of 'living off immoral earnings' in 1912 and many convictions regards street gambling (my old dad was a bookies runner as a child of about 14) and a nineteen year old girl drowned herself in a canal in 1902. All of these people were living in Bayonne Road at the time.

Then, in respect to my old house, back in September of the year 1900, a Mr Thomas Toons was living in my house at number 48 Bayonne Road. After tragically losing two of his children, he finally gave way to the demon drink. He'd been working for the previous eighteen months at a firm in Munster Road, Messrs Batey & Co. He fell on hard times and was charged with embezzlement. He pleaded guilty and was sentenced to one month imprisonment. Sadly, there was even a suicide in my house at one time as, back in March of the year 1889, Mrs Elizabeth Smith, at just aged 42, was the widow of John Smith, a well known postman. She also succumbed to the demon drink and had been lodging at 48 Bayonne Road for three years.

She'd tired of being addicted to drink so she ended her life by taking two ounces of Laudanum. For the last two weeks of her life she only drank Brandy. If walls could talk, I'm sure my old house would have even more to say.

Sadly, I never got to meet my grandfather as he'd died a few years before I was born. My nan, on the other hand, certainly met me, as she was alive until I was about 18 months old. I like to think she sat me on her knee a few times. I may not quite have know her, but I take comfort in the fact that she knew me. Here is a sketch of the photo I have of me with Mr Augustus (Harry) Webb & Mrs Violet Webb and their poodle Pepe. I am standing on the wall of number 8 Bayonne Road (my grandparents old house) Mr & Mrs Webb moved into the house after my nan died. Mr Webb died in 1970 and Mrs Webb, one of the last residents to leave Bayonne Road before demolition, died in 1976.

# BAYONNE ROAD

*T*he January snow changed life's pace from fast to slow,
   and the children played and played until they froze.
And the snowmen they did grow, stretched in never ending row
with eyes of coal and a carrot for a nose.


Then as February came, our mums and dads did just the same
   throwing snowballs, with hands of ice and chilblained feet.
   With the neighbours playing too, their problems seemed so far
and few
   times were hard, but friendly, living in our street.


March winds blew hard and fast, and the snow it didn't last,
   waking up the Daffs and tortoises and things.
   All the Hares were dancing crazy, with the whiff of new born Daisies,
   and soon we saw, such is the beauty of the spring.

April showers washed the drains, and the smells swam through them with the rain, and it made the two cars down my street all clean and shiny.

Not like now, the rain brings grime, which sort of happened over time, unlike my unpolluted world when I was tiny.


Then the sun pops out to say, in the merry month of May,

how are things my friend its a while since I've seen you.

Let me rid you of these clouds and bring back hoards of sun tanned crowds,

and I'll offer everyone around a sky of blue.


Four weeks passed and all to soon, we found we were in the month of June, and my skin was red apart from my feet and hands.

We'd all been to Brighton Pier, and even supped our daddies beer.

Some years we even got to go to Camber Sands.


Then I soon found I was peeling, picking my skin was a lovely feeling,

it was July and thats when it happened as a rule.

Life back then was full of fun and it seemed we saw so much more sun,

and we'd look forward to the six weeks we got off school.


August always makes me sad for the love that I once had,

and the years that passed as I grew into a man.

Now that I have grown much older, am I wiser, am I bolder ?

I`m not sure, but honest, I do the best I can.

Life had never been the same, since that cold September rain,
    when the good lord chose our dad to to be his friend.
    As for those he left behind, I guess we didn't really mind,
    but we knew mums broken heart would never mend.


And as October rain had come, eight years on, he took our mum
    he let her rest and gave her freedom from her pain.
    We all knew that it was good, she had to go, we understood,
    so that they could be together once again.


Then the dark November clouds filled the sky and wouldn't move,
    and they stayed there for the following weeks to come.
    With the new year getting near, and my lack of festive cheer,
    how would Xmas be without my dad and mum.


Then the clouds all went away on that cold December day,
    and the sun shone so it freed us from our fears.
    'Cause we knew that they were there, and we knew they'd always
care.
    And in our dreams at night, they'll visit us for years.
    © John E Bath

∾

# RAINBOW BRIDGE

*J*ust this side of heaven, is a place called the Rainbow Bridge.
When an animal dies that has been especially close to
someone here,
that pet goes to the Rainbow Bridge.
There are meadows and hills for all of our special friends
so they can run and play together.
There is plenty of food, water and sunshine, and our friends
are warm and comfortable.

All the animals who had been ill and old are restored to health
and vigor; those who were hurt or maimed are made whole and
strong again, just as we remember them in our dreams of days
and times gone by.
The animals are happy and content, except for one small thing;
They each miss someone very special to them,
who had been left behind.
They all run and play together, but the day comes when
one suddenly stops and looks into the distance.
His bright eyes are intent; His eager body quivers.

Suddenly he begins to run from the group, flying over
the green green grass, his legs carrying him faster and faster.
You have been spotted, and when you and your special friend
finally meet, you cling together in joyous reunion,
never to be parted again. The happy kisses rain upon your face;
your hands again caress the beloved head,
and you look once more into the trusting eyes of your pet,
So long gone from your life but never absent from your heart.


Then you cross the Rainbow Bridge together.


-Anonymous

~

# FAMOUS HAMMERSMITHONIANS

*L*ike many other London boroughs, Hammersmith can proudly say it's once been the home for a whole host of celebrities. From world champion boxers to award-winning actors, the borough has produced an array of talent which people all over the world have come to love.

And you probably don't realise how many people you regularly see on TV or read about in the newspaper are actually from the area. So with this in mind, I've compiled a list of 12 celebrities which you may not know are from Hammersmith.

## Sacha Baron Cohen

Best known for his roles in hit-comedy's Borat and Bruno, Sacha Baron Cohen was born in Hammersmith and grew up in the area in his early life. He studied at Haberdashers' Aske's Boys' School, in Elstree, before studying at the University of Cambridge. As well as appearing in Borat and Bruno, he has starred in Ali G and 2012 film The Dictator.

**Joe Calzaghe:**

Former super middleweight world champion Joe Calzaghe was born in Hammersmith but only lived in the area for two years. When he was just two-years-old, his family moved to Wales where he was educated and grew up. The boxer, who retired in 2008, is the longest-reigning super-middleweight world champion in boxing history, having held the WBO title for more than 10 years, making 21 successful defence.

**Sebastian Coe:**

The man who set three world records over the one-mile distance during his incredible track career was born in Hammersmith. Seb Coe, who won Olympic gold over 1,500m in the 1980 and 1984 games, moved to Warwickshire when he was just one-year-old, and later moved to Sheffield when he was a teenager. He was heavily involved when London held the 2012 Olympics, and is now the president of the International Association of Athletics Federations.

**James May:**

James has lived in the borough for most of his life Former Top Gear presenter James May was actually born in Bristol but has lived in Hammersmith for most of his life. The Cross Keys pub, on Black Lion Lane, is said to be the presenter's local, where he regularly pops in for a bite to eat or drink. But don't tell him I told you. Most recently, James became a co-presenter for television series The Grand Tour, alongside former Top Gear colleagues Jeremy Clarkson and Richard Hammond.

**Tom Hardy:**

The actor best known for his role in 2010 film 'Inception' was born in Hammersmith. He continued to live in the borough but studied at Tower House School, in Richmond upon Thames, and Duff Miller Sixth Form College, in Kensington. In a successful career the 40-year-old has starred in a number of movies including Star Trek: Nemesis, The Revenant, Legend and Dunkirk.

**Lily Allen:**

Singer and songwriter Lily Allen was born in Hammersmith.

**Stuart Pearce:**

Former West Ham United, Manchester City and England defender Stuart Pearce was born and grew up in the area. But he lived a bit further out, attending Fryent Primary School, in Kingsbury, and then Claremont High School, in Kenton. More recently he was the assistant manager to David Moyes at West Ham, but left his role last month.

**George Groves:**

The current WBA (Super) super-middleweight champion was born in Hammersmith and grew up in King Street. The boxer, who trained at Dale Youth Boxing club when he was younger, has won 28 of his 31 fights during his career, and has won by KO 20 times. He famously lost to fellow boxer Carl Froch in front of 80,000 fans at Wembley Stadium in 2014.

**Benedict Cumberbatch:**

The successful actor, best known for playing Sherlock Holmes in BBC crime series Sherlock, was born in Hammersmith but grew up in Kensington. He attended Harrow School when he was younger, and once turned down the chance to play his first acting role in a school production of William Shakespeare play Hamlet, instead choosing to focus on his A-Levels. While the actor now lives near Hampstead Heath, his parents are believed to still live near to the Duke and Duchess of Cambridge's home, Kensington Palace.

**Hugh Grant:**

Well known actor Hugh Grant was born in Hammersmith before moving to Hounslow as a child, attending The William Hogarth School, in Chiswick. The actor and film producer is probably best known for his roles in Love Actually, Bridget Jones's Diary and Paddington 2. He later moved to Harrington Gardens, in South Kensington and then to Fulham Road in Chelsea.

**Miranda Hart:**

Although born in Torquay, comedian Miranda Hart has lived in Hammersmith for most of her life.

She has admitted in the past she lives to walk along the Chiswick towpath and over Hammersmith Bridge as a past time. While she has also published a number of books, Miranda has starred as Miss Hannigan in the West End production of Annie.

And last, but by no means least….

### John Bath, Composer and Conductor, born 1915 - died 2004

Vocal parts of a lost Mass, written for the Catholic Church in Rye by the composer John Bath, have been found a week after his own Requiem was held there. A significant figure in both the church, where he was choirmaster and organist in the 1940s and 1950s, and the Rye Singers, he wrote hundreds of pieces, the Mass of St. Anthony of Padua being Opus 467; it was found by Sheila Miller who remembered it in the days after his funeral. A search is now on for the part scored for the organ.

When John Bath died he was, at 89, the oldest surviving chorister of the Westminster Cathedral Choir School, where he was educated in the 1920s, and sang at their re-union in 2003. The current choirmaster and organist at St. Anthonys, Professor Trevor Ling of the Royal Academy of music, himself spent more than 20 years with the Cathedral choir and led the singing during the RequiemMass.

John Hubert Giffin Bath was born in London on 2 July 1915, son of the composer and conductor Hubert Bath, who is still remembered for his popular work "Cornish Rhapsody".

When war broke out in 1939 John joined the Army and served with a film unit; after the war he worked primarily as a composer of music for films, including one about life on board an aircraft carrier. The music was played by Royal Marine bandsmen and matched to the film under his supervision at Ealing Studios. On other occasions he flew to newly liberated France, and sometimes Germany, putting together an orchestra to record his music. Altogether, he wrote hundreds of works, including wedding marches for members of his own family. For some time, he was, on the recommendation of Sir Malcolm Sargent, conductor of the BBC's West of England Light Orchestra. After leaving Rye, where they lived in Mermaid Street and are still remembered, the family moved to Hollywood via Canada. His best-known music in Britain is the theme music from the Canadian Television series "The Forest Rangers", 45rpm records of which were distributed to the people attending his Requiem Mass on September 2nd 2004; it was celebrated by the parish priest, Fr. Aidan Walsh OFM (Conv).

Apart from the composing and conducting, he was involved in amateur, and sometimes not so amateur dramatics. It was while playing with the Curtene Players in Hastings that he met his wife Iris.

After working for the British Foreign Office, Iris became a professional actress and appeared in a number of Hollywood films. They married in London in 1958. ( the year I entered the world) It was at about this time that he conducted the mysterious Hastings Symphony Orchestra in a performance of Borodins Symphony No 2, released on the Allegro label as ALG3048.

Soon after John and Iris Bath returned to the UK, he died unexpectedly in the Conquest Hospital.

One son, Tristan, is on the diplomatic staff of the US Embassy in Warsaw; the other children Piers, Perpetua, and Felicity live in California. All were present to support their mother at the funeral, Piers and Tristan helping to carry the coffin into the church.

Of course, it is not beyond the realms of possibility that we might be related somewhere along the line, but as of this present moment in time, I'm none the wiser.

~

# HISTORY OF THE BIG REC

This triangular site owned by the Ecclesiastical Commissioners, was bought by the Fulham Vestry in 1891 in order to provide recreational space for the growing population in the area. Funding was received from the LCC and it opened as a Fulham Recreation Ground, its name later changed to Lillie Road Recreation Ground.

Known locally as the Big Rec, the park originally had railings along the central path and a bandstand, gymnasium and gardens. An extension beyond the east wall was added as part of the redevelopment of the Fulham riverside in the 1970s, which has a grass area with raised beds and some play equipment.

Previous / Other name: Fulham Recreation Ground

Site location: Lillie Road, Fulham

Postcode: SW6

Type of site: Public Park

Borough: Hammersmith & Fulham

Open to public? Yes

Opening times: 7.30am - dusk

The road and recreation ground get their name from Sir John Scott Lillie, a veteran of the Peninsular War who owned land in Fulham and began development of what is the eastern end of Lillie Road in 1826. He lived at a house called The Hermitage set in extensive grounds on the corner of Lillie and North End Road, later built over by coal yards. Lillie was also an inventor and responsible for an early machine gun, which became known as the Lillie Rifle.

A gardener called Sandell once had a business here, resulting in it gaining the name Sandell's Corner. In the C17th the land where the recreation ground was later laid out was an orchard and gravel pits in the ownership Lady Pye, whose son Sir Nicholas Crispe was a wealthy trader in goods and slaves. Crispe built Brandenburgh House on the Fulham riverside, and after his death in 1666 at his behest his embalmed heart was buried in Hammersmith chapel-at-ease, later St Paul's Hammersmith (q.v.), although his body was buried at St Mildred's Bread Street, only reunited when St Mildred's churchyard was cleared in 1898 and his remains brought to Hammersmith.

The recreation ground is extensively used for sport as a result of which the grass has suffered and there are large tracts of asphalt. A mural on the sports centre was repainted in July 1996. On the north-west corner of the site is a kiosk and public conveniences, the lodge now used for alternative healthcare. There are good London plane trees in the park. The railings along Fulham Palace Road were set back to produce a grass verge along the road and shrubs are now being planted in the area.

~

# HISTORY OF FFC

ounded in 1879, Fulham is one of the oldest British football clubs. The Club was born when a school teacher and church-warden formed a team for local boys at Fulham-St Andrew's Church. Fulham won the Southern League in the seasons 1905-06 and 1906-07, and joined the Second Division of the Football League in the following season. Although cricket initially took the priority, seven years later, the team won their first silverware, the West London Amateur Cup, beating St Matthew's 2-1 in the Final.

Fulham itself dates back to at least the eighth century. The Bishop of London acquired the manor of Fulham in 704 and Danish invaders landed here in 879. A fishing village grew up in the vicinity of the present Putney Bridge station and Fulham High Street was in existence by 1391, when it was called Burystrete. The west tower of All Saints Church was built around 1440. The earliest of the surviving buildings of Fulham Palace date from around 1480, when it became one of the bish-op's country retreats.

Medieval villages grew up at three distinct locations in Fulham in addition to the thriving old town: Parsons Green, Walham Green and North End. Fulham Palace became the bishop's main residence in the 18th century.

Among the gentlemen's retreats built in the Georgian era were Hurlingham House, later home to the prestigious sports club, and Lord Craven's cottage orné north of the palace, built in 1780. The earlier Peterborough House was rebuilt around the same time.

Fulham town hall was built for Fulham vestry in 1888–90

Over the course of the 19th century industry filled the reclaimed marshland of Sands End. Elsewhere, terraces of suburban housing rolled out across the former market gardens and gentlemen's estates from the 1870s.

North End was rebranded West Kensington and Fulham Broadway, at Walham Green, became Fulham's administrative and shopping centre. Peterborough House was demolished to make way for a pleasing estate that bears its name.

Fulham Football Club built a permanent home on the site of Craven Cottage in 1896, 17 years after the club's foundation. In April 1904 Fulham Theatre held the first public experiment in 'talking pictures' with the aid of a phonographic soundtrack.

Much of Fulham's new housing was built for the lower middle classes but by the 1920s large parts of the district had become wholly working class in character.

Before and after the Second World War the borough council added several housing estates, most visibly on the eastern side of West Kensington.

Fulham Palace ceased to be the bishop's official residence in 1973 and most of its grounds were opened to the public. Gentrification since this time has been so widespread throughout the district that it is hard to believe that Fulham had a poor reputation 60 years ago. The deserted industrial wasteland by the Thames at Sands End has provided the principal zone of opportunity for large-scale developers, beginning with Chelsea Harbour in the 1980s and reaching a crescendo at Imperial Wharf.

In underworld slang from the 16th to the late 18th centuries 'fulhams' were loaded dice. The word was also written as 'fullams', and it is not certain that there was originally any connection with this place – although Fulham was once a noted resort of 'sharpers'.

Fulham stoneware was a hard ceramic ware, typically brown-glazed, made at Fulham Pottery from 1672.

A Fulham virgin was an ironic 19th-century euphemism for a prostitute. The name may have been inspired by the proximity of Cremorne Gardens, a resort that acquired a reputation as "a nursery of every kind of vice."

# HISTORY OF HAMMERSMITH

*S*cene of the grisly murders of six women in the early 1960s. The 'Hammersmith nude murders' is the name of a series of six murders in 1964 and 1965. The victims, all believed to be sex workers, were found undressed in or near the River Thames, leading the press to nickname the killer 'Jack the Stripper' (imho a somewhat distastefully obvious reference to the Whitechapel murderer, 'Jack the Ripper' of the late 1880s) Two earlier murders, committed in West London in 1959 and 1963, have also been linked by some investigators to the same perpetrator.

Despite 'intense media interest and one of the biggest manhunts in Scotland Yard's history' the case is unsolved. Forensic evidence gathered at the time is believed to have been destroyed or lost.

On a more lighter note, Hammersmith is a strategically significant commercial and cultural centre, located on the north bank of the Thames one-and-a-half miles west of Kensington.

Prehistoric pottery, flints and a leaf-shaped arrowhead have been found on the embankment and there is also evidence of Roman habitation. Hammersmith developed as a Saxon fishing village and its name (which probably refers to the presence of a hammer smithy or forge) was first recorded in 1294.

A foreshore of gravel, rather than the more common marsh, made Hammersmith a healthy retreat for jaded Londoners from the Middle Ages onwards and a chapel of ease, later St Paul's church, was built in 1631. Further west, boat builders, lead mills and malthouses clustered around the outlet of Stamford Creek into the Thames.

Catherine of Braganza, queen consort of Charles II, came to live on Upper Mall in 1687 after she was widowed, and several fine villas were later built by the river here. Charles II had a few merry nights with Nell Gwynn in Sanford Manor House in Fulham. Fulham Gas Works was built in the grounds of the manor in 1826.

A ribbon of houses flanked the road to London by the early 19th century and Hammersmith Bridge opened in 1827, stimulating development on both sides of the river. Hammersmith gained parochial independence from Fulham in 1834.

Away from the riverside, a poverty-stricken settlement evolved at Brook Green during the mid-19th century, since when its reputation has risen considerably. The Hammersmith and City Railway arrived in 1864. In the late 19th century King Street became the district's main shopping centre and the Metropolitan Board of Works opened Ravenscourt Park to the public.

**The Ark:**

Much of Hammersmith's architectural heritage was lost in the middle decades of the 20th century as the district became increasingly urbanised but some important examples have survived, especially by the riverside. Subsequent gentrification has rehabilitated Victorian streets such as those in Brackenbury Village.

Hammersmith flyover – dubbed 'the gateway to west London' – was built in 1961. As a five year old child, I walked over it from one end to the other with a boy from my street. His name was Chris Povey. Someone who drove past and saw us went and told my dad. By the time I got to the other end he was there waiting for me and took us back to our homes in Bayonne Road.

The flyover is now overlooked by a thing named the 'Ark'. A copper and glass monstrosity, sorry, building, that is among several office blocks in the vicinity of Hammersmith Broadway. This is one of London's busiest traffic junctions, with a bus station and two separate tube stations, plus a large shopping mall at its heart. Charing Cross Hospital moved to its present home on the Fulham Palace Road in 1973. Maggie's cancer centre, the first of its kind in England, opened at the hospital in 2008.

Hammersmith has three noteworthy arts and entertainment venues:

**The Lyric:**

a 19th-century auditorium and a studio theatre encased in concrete.

**The Apollo:**

Which I have added some extra information under its earlier name, Hammersmith Odeon. It is a former cinema that now hosts major rock gigs and stand-up comedy shows, and:

**The Riverside Studios:**

The Riverside Studios, a cinema and performing arts venue, was refurbished in 2017. Sadly, the legendary ballroom, the Hammersmith Palais, closed in 2007 and was demolished in 2012.

The riverbank west of Hammersmith Bridge is lined with long-established inns. The Rutland and the Blue Anchor (They are often seen at the beginning of the tv show 'Minder', are on Lower Mall, which Nikolaus Pevsner commends as 'Hammersmith's best street'.

On Upper Mall, James Thomson wrote the words to 'Rule Britannia' in an upstairs room at The Dove pub. One of its bars is reputed to be Britain's smallest, with less than 33 square feet of floor space. Beyond the Dove you'll come to the Old Ship and then the Black Lion. From there on in you soon stumble into Chiswick.

JMW Turner lived on Upper Mall from 1808 to 1814. On the same street, Francis Ronalds invented the electric telegraph in 1816, in the garden of a house in which designer-craftsman William Morris lived from the age of 45 until his death in 1896.

Morris called the house Kelmscott after his Oxfordshire home. He also gave the same name to a publishing firm that he founded. Gustav Holst conducted the Hammersmith socialist choir at Kelmscott and composed an orchestral prelude and scherzo entitled Hammersmith. There was another composer who hailed from Hammersmith. Blessed with, of all names, the handsome monica of, 'John Bath' (Alas, no relation) Born 2nd Just 1915 in Hammersmith, he died on the 23rd September 2004 in Hastings aged 89. Amongst many other scores, he composed the music to one of the episodes of the old 'Dick Barton' tv series.

Talking of tv series, the BBC2 sitcom Bottom, which ran from 1991 through to 1995, created by and starring Adrian Edmondson and Rik Mayall) was set in a squalid flat in the fictional Mafeking Parade (or Terrace), Hammersmith. Following Mayall's untimely death in 2014, a memorial bench was installed at the junction of Queen Caroline Street and Hammersmith Bridge Road.

~

# NINE THINGS YOU MIGHT NOT KNOW
## ABOUT HAMMERSMITH BRIDGE

1:

*I*t was the first suspension bridge over the Thames

The original Hammersmith bridge opened in 1827, and was designed by William Tierney Clark.

The first Hammersmith Bridge in 1828.

It was the first suspension bridge over the River Thames: that is a bridge where the deck is hung below suspension cables on vertical suspenders.

There were concerns about the strength of the bridge as early as the 1850s. Crowds loved to watch the boat race from this particular vantage point, halfway through the course: when crowds on the bridge hit around the 11,000 mark in the late 1860s, the bridge swayed from side to side as people flocked to the sides to see the race.

Crowds on Hammersmith Bridge during the 1866 Boat Race.

By the 1870s, it became evident that it was not strong enough to support the volume of traffic going across it; it took until 1884 for a replacement to start being built.

## 2: The current bridge was designed by Sir Joseph Bazalgette

It was opened by the Prince of Wales on 11th June 1887. With most of the structure being built of wrought iron. It is 700 feet long and 43 feet wide. It cost £87,117 to build.

The current Hammersmith Bridge is very ornate with wrought-iron parapets, mild steel chain links and air draught gauges both up and down stream. The decorative iron blocks that support the walkway sit on squat, clustered 'Doric columns' on stone piers in the river.

## 3: The lowdown on London's lowest bridge

How low can you go? If you're on Hammersmith Bridge, the answer is: very low. Hammersmith Bridge boasts a water clearance of just 12 feet at high tide, making it the lowest bridge over the river Thames. It is so low that the river path only just fits below it on the Barnes bank, and is prone to flooding.

## 4: It's pretty crest-heavy

Hammersmith Bridge features not one but seven coats of arms. The septet of heraldic decoration features the present Royal Arms of the United Kingdom in the centre.

Around the edge, the others are (clockwise from the left): the coat of arms of the City of London; Kent; Guildford; the original coat of arms of the City of Westminster (with the portcullis); the coat of arms of Colchester; and Middlesex (in its original form without the crown).

In previous years, these seven crests have been painted in their varied colours: today they're all green and gold, but some have called for them to be returned to their former glory.

## 5: It's London's weakest bridge

Unfortunately, Bazalgette's 130-year-old bridge just isn't strong enough for today's modern traffic. Weak bridge: Hammersmith Bridge struggles to support modern traffic.

Indeed, the bridge was already too weak 40 years ago.

**Hammersmith Bridge 1970-1975**

Hammersmith Bridge currently operates under severe weight restrictions. Only one bus in each direction permitted on the bridge at any one time. It's an ongoing problem: there have been substantial improvement works in 1998, 2000, 2016, and 2017.

## 6: It hasn't always been green

As you can see from the video above, Hammersmith Bridge was painted in a rather fetching mishmash of pastels during the last century. But the bridge was repainted green in 2000, back to its original hue following advice from English Heritage.

The bridge was covered in a pale pink undercoat for the first year of its life, but then painted green in accordance with Bazalgette's plans. And if anyone's told you Hammersmith Bridge is painted green and gold to match the nearby Harrods furniture depository, we're fairly sure they're wrong: the latter opened in 1894, more than five years after Bazalgette painted his bridge green.

## 7: The decorative bits aren't just flouncy additions

In fact, bits of the bridge's intricate design add to its performance.

For example, the decorative copulas on top of the towers are actually functional, acting as protective covers for the bearings for the unique eye-bar chains that hold up the Bridge.

## 8: Hammersmith Bridge's heroic plaque

Near midnight on 27 December 1919, a Lieutenant Charles Campbell Wood from Bloemfontein in South Africa, dived into the Thames from the upstream footway of Hammersmith Bridge to rescue a drowning woman.

They both survived the ordeal, but Campbell Wood died of tetanus contracted from his injuries, and died two weeks later. His bravery is commemorated with a plaque on Hammersmith Bridge.

### 9: It's been bombed twice

Hammersmith Bridge has been the target of two bombs: once by the IRA in 1939, and once by the Provisional IRA in 2000.

1939: The first bomb was spotted by Maurice Childs, a hairdresser from Chiswick. Walking home at one in the morning, Childs spotted a smoking suitcase lying on the bridge's walkway. He quickly threw the bag in the river: the resulting explosion sent up a 60-foot column of water. Moments later, a second device exploded causing girders on the west side of the bridge to collapse.

Childs was later awarded an MBE for his quick-thinking.


2000: The second incident occurred on June 1st 2000. At 4.30am, the bridge was damaged by a Real IRA bomb planted underneath the Barnes span.

~

# HAMMERSMITH ODEON

*T*he venue was opened in 1932 as the Gaumont Palace and seated nearly 3,500 people. It was designed by Robert Cromie in the Art Deco style. In 1962, the building was renamed Hammersmith Odeon, a name many people still use for the venue. It became a Grade II Listed Building in 1990. The venue was later refurbished and renamed Labatt's Apollo following a sponsorship deal with Labatt Brewing Company (1993 or 1994).

In 2002, the venue was again renamed, this time to Carling Apollo after Carling Apollo brewery struck a deal with the owners, US-based Clear Channel Entertainment (spun off as Live Nation (Venues) UK Ltd in 2005). The venue's listing was upgraded to Grade II status in 2005. In 2003, the stalls seats were made removable and now some concerts have full seating whilst others have standing-only in the stalls. In the latter format the venue can accommodate around 5,000 people. The event was marked by rock band AC/DC playing an exclusive one-off concert and only charging £10 per ticket. All 5,000 tickets sold out in 4 minutes.

In 2006, the venue reverted to its former name, the Hammersmith Apollo. In 2007, the original 1932 Compton pipe organ, still present from the building's days as a cinema, was restored. The building then changed hands and was bought by the MAMA Group.

On 14 January 2009, a placing announcement by HMV Group revealed that by selling additional shares, the company would raise money to fund a joint venture with the MAMA Group, to run eleven live music venues across the United Kingdom, including the Hammersmith Apollo. As a result, the venue was named HMV Apollo from 2009 until 2012.

The venue was sold by HMV Group in May 2012 to AEG Live. In 2013, the venue was closed for an extensive refurbishment which was carried out by award-winning architect Foster Wilson. The venue reopened as the Eventime Apollo on 7 September 2013, with a concert performance by Selena Gomez.

**The Compton pipe organ**.

The original 1932 Compton pipe organ is still present at the Apollo and was fully restored to playing condition in 2007. It has a four-manual console which rises through the stage on a new lift and about 1,200 organ pipes housed in large chambers above the front stalls ceiling. Having fallen into disrepair, the organ was disconnected in the 1990s and the console removed from the building.

At the insistence of English Heritage and the local council, however, it was reinstated and the entire organ restored. At a launch party, on 25 July 2007, an invited audience and media representatives witnessed a recital by Richard Hills.

Many bands have released live albums, videos or DVDs of concerts held at the Apollo, such as Queen, Black Sabbath, Rush, Hawkwind, Iron Maiden, Celtic Frost, Kings of Leon, Tears for Fears, Dire Straits, Frank Zappa, Sophie Ellis-Bextor, David Bowie, Bruce Springsteen and the E Street Band, Erasure, Spear of Destiny, Motörhead, and Robbie Williams.

In September 1979 Gary Numan recorded his Touring Principle show at the venue. Kate Bush released a video and record EP of her concerts at the Odeon from her first tour in 1979. Duran Duran recorded at the Hammersmith Odeon on 16 November 1982 and released *Live at Hammersmith '82!*. Depeche Mode made one of its first concert videos for a Danish television at the Hammersmith on 25 October 1982. Alchemy: Dire Straits Live was recorded at the Odeon.

Of course many other bands have played here. In 1963 The Rolling Stones first ever concert tour was a 'package tour' headlined by the Everly Brothers and Bo Diddley. The tour commenced on 29 September and concluded on 3 November 1963 at the Hammersmith Odeon. They performed two ten-minute shows at every one of the 30 days.

The Beatles were the first band to play at the Odeon. Starting on Christmas Eve, they played six shows between 24th - 31st 1964. They had Christmas Day off and the 27th (my dads birthday)

If you ever get the chance to watch the Beatles film 'A Hard Days Night' (a phrase coined by Ringo) Check out the scene, about forty five minutes into the film. All four of the Beatles are seen running down from a rather large, rather high, fire escape. Even though, once they reach the bottom, they run out onto an airfield to board the awaiting helicopter, the fire escape is in fact, the one at the back of Hammersmith Odeon.

It's only right that I mention that Blondie played there a few times, and of course Tom Waits did too. He played three nights there between 19th - 21st November 1987. Then, on September 10th 2004 the tickets for his return to the Odeon sold out in thirty minutes. Unfortunately, to my great loss, I never got to see him. However, I did see Blondie perform there in 1978 and Status Quo in 1977.

~

# KING STREET, HAMMERSMITH

*A*s a lad, back in 1970, I worked in Hedges the butchers. It was a little shop in Hammersmith Market which was off King Street. Then, after a few months had passed, when they were moved out to a shop a few miles away, I got myself a job on George Throwers' fruit and veg stall which was just outside.

For a few weekends you would see me, or should that be, 'hear' me, on a Saturday morning shouting out; 'C'mon ladies, arffa panda cherries, one and six.' or 'Arffa duzzun bananas, only arrfa crahn.' Even though I never actually spoke with a plum in me mouth, I did like to eat them occasionally. Then 'they' came in and did what 'they' are good at with their much overly used dreaded 'R' word as a means weaponry. The R word standing for regeneration. Now, just like many other places, it's all changed, and not necessarily for the better, it rarely is. I think the market is still there, but smaller, much smaller.

Like lots of people, I used to buy most of my albums from the big record shop on the broadway, at the start of King Street. I remember the first time I ever went in there. I asked the man at the counter if they had anything by The Doors. He said 'Yeh, a fire extinguisher and a bucket of sand.' I say I bought all my albums from there. That's not entirely true as I went to one in Putney High Street in around 1972. I'd gone in there to buy Sparky's Magic Piano but they didn't have it in stock.

The man there suggested that if I liked Sparky, I might like Tubby the Tuba, and as a means of consolation I might, just might, like to buy that one instead. They had a couple of those booths where you could put on a pair of headphones to listen to a sample of the album before you decided to buy it, or not as the case may be. Little ol me went into the booth, put on the headphones and had a listen to Tubby the Tuba. They must have thought they had a right one that day. I was about 32 at the time, no that's a lie, I was only 29. At least I managed to stop myself from bopping my head along to the music.

A few years later I finally managed to regain some street cred, not that I'd lost any as I don't think I ever had any in the first place. I'd gone into the record shop in King Street and picked up three different Tom Waits album sleeves. I took them to the counter to ask if they had them in stock. The fella there called his assistant over and showed him what I was buying. They both nodded in agreement and commented how cool it was to have someone actually come in and ask for a bit of 'class' for a change. I paid for the three albums and as I walked away from the counter I could have sworn I'd grown two inches taller. Walking out the door that day, I held my head aloft, I felt five foot six tall.

ps I still have that Tubby the Tuba album, but not once did I go back to that shop in Putney High Street.

King Street, being the principal shopping street of Hammersmith Broadway, runs west from Hammersmith Broadway to Stamford Brook, there it meets Chiswick High Road and Goldhawk Road. Back in the 1970s, my shoes were mainly bought from a little shop half way up that street, it was called Shelleys aka 'The Direct Shoe Supply'. I got my very first pair of Dr Marten 1460 boots from them. I loved those boots. Cherry red with air cushion soles. The only downside was the sole wore out too quickly, probably on account of the fact that I wore them day in and day out. Over time, I bought my first pair of Tassel Loafers then Ivy Brogues, all from Shelleys.

What with my Two-Tone Tonic trowzizz, Ben Sherman dicky dirt, felt collared navy blue, single breasted Crombie overcoat with red silk hanky (to match the lining) poking out from the front top pocket, I must have looked quite the dandy. Maybe not.

~

This was a turnpike road from 1717 and during the course of the 18th century it acquired houses, inns, stables and Cromwell's brewery. Before it was covered over, Stamford Brook used to open out into a creek near the brewery. King Street gained its present name around 1794.Rivercourt Methodist church was built on the corner Rivercourt Road and King Street in 1874–5. Shops began to line the street towards the end of the 19th century. King Street was widened in the 1930s, when Hammersmith town hall was built and many of the original shops were demolished. The construction of the A4 two decades later relieved the street of its role as part of the Great West Road.

In more recent times, the big-name stores are clustered towards the eastern end, including those within the Ashcroft Square and Kings Mall precincts. In January 2020 the Kings Mall was bought by the Swedish furniture retailer, Ikea.

The Lyric theatre is a focal arts venue for west London. A gilt and velvet auditorium has been rebuilt inside this 1970s concrete structure. Lyric Square host a farmers' market on Thursdays. It's particularly noted for its freshly prepared takeaway food.

The Latymer arts centre, at 237 King Street, is a private facility for Latymer upper school with a four-storey atrium serving as a theatre foyer and art gallery.

The Salutation Inn was built in 1910 on the site of a Victorian pub of the same name. Awarding it a grade 11 listing, Historic England says this is 'a rare and complete survival in London of the use of lustrous finish faience tiling.' It's a very pleasant place inside too, with several original details intact. The western part of King Street has a strong Polish presence, with retailers, and a social and cultural centre that incorporates a theatre and a restaurant.

I believe, at one time during the 1960s, the singer, Arnold George Dorsey MBE (born 2 May 1936) lived above 'Times Furnishing' in King Street. His impression of Jerry Lewis prompted friends to begin calling him 'Gerry Dorsey', a name he worked under for almost ten years.

In 1965, Dorsey teamed up with Gordon Mills, his former room-mate whilst living in Bayswater, who had become a music impresario and the manager of Tom Jones. Gordon Mills, aware that Dorsey had been struggling for several years to become successful in the music industry, suggested a name-change to the more arresting, Engelbert Humperdinck.

The name being borrowed from the 19th century German composer of operas such as Hansel and Gretel. Dorsey adopted the name professionally but not legally. Mills arranged a new deal for him with Decca Records, and he has been performing under this name ever since.

©John E Bath

～

# GUNNERSBURY PARK

*H*eading out from Hammersmith and Fulham, just a bit further west of Chiswick, is Gunnersbury. Gunnersbury is one of the few places in London to have been named after a woman, in this case Gunnhildr, whose manor this was.

Gunnersbury House was a Palladian mansion built in the mid-17th century for Sir John Maynard, the king's principal serjeant-at-law. Princess Amelia, daughter of George II, made the villa her summer residence from 1762 to 1786.

The estate was sold in 1800 and the house was demolished and replaced by Gunnersbury Park and Gunnersbury House, later called the Large Mansion and the Small Mansion.

In 1835 Gunnersbury Park was acquired and then enlarged by the banker Nathan Mayer Rothschild. His nephew Leopold de Rothschild bought Gunnersbury House in 1889 and put it to use as a guest house for visitors to Gunnersbury Park, who included Edward VII.

After Leopold's death in 1917 the estate was split up. Part was sold for building, while the local boroughs bought the mansions and 186 acres of parkland.

The Large Mansion is home to Gunnersbury Park Museum, which displays Ealing and Hounslow's local history collections. The Small Mansion is mostly falling into disrepair.

Throughout the summers of the 1960s, I spent many a happy day out here with my sisters and a few of my cousins. Upon our very first visit we came across the Potomac Boat House. A mid-C19 Gothic folly tower, converted from a tile kiln and situated on the southern shore of Potomac Lake. Although the huge wooden front door was locked shut, we soon discovered a secret entrance where we gained access down by the waters edge.

It looked like it was designed with small boats in mind where they could row into the lower lever of the folly. With our somewhat moistened feet, we often went inside to play for a while before setting off and continuing the rest of our adventure in other parts of this huge, magnificent park.

In 2014 the Heritage Lottery Fund and Big Lottery Fund made a grant for the restoration of, and improvements to the landscape and buildings of Gunnersbury Park. The museum reopened in June 2018 and the overall 'transformation' is due for completion in around 2026.

Gunnersbury station (originally Brentford Road) was rebuilt in 1966 with an 18 storey office block above, now occupied by the British Standards Institution.

The Russian Orthodox Cathedral stands on Harvard Road, just south of the station. It was built in 1998 in the traditional 'Pskov' style, with an onion-shaped dome painted in blue with gold stars.

Gunnersbury Triangle is a six-acre nature reserve on Bollo Lane, situated between railway lines. It has birch and willow woodland with an attractive pond, marsh and meadow.

# I F

*If you can keep your head when all about you*
      *Are losing theirs and blaming it on you;*
*If you can trust yourself when all men doubt you,*
*But make allowance for their doubting too:*
*If you can wait and not be tired by waiting,*
*Or, being lied about, don't deal in lies,*
*Or being hated don't give way to hating,*
*And yet don't look too good, nor talk too wise;*


*If you can dream- -and not make dreams your master;*
      *If you can think- -and not make thoughts your aim,*
      *If you can meet with Triumph and Disaster*
      *And treat those two impostors just the same:.*
      *If you can bear to hear the truth you've spoken*
      *Twisted by knaves to make a trap for fools,*
      *Or watch the things you gave your life to, broken,*
      *And stoop and build'em up with worn-out tools;*

*If you can make one heap of all your winnings*
*And risk it on one turn of pitch-and-toss,*
*And lose, and start again at your beginnings,*
*And never breathe a word about your loss:*
*If you can force your heart and nerve and sinew*
*To serve your turn long after they are gone,*
*And so hold on when there is nothing in you*
*Except the Will which says to them: 'Hold on! '*

*If you can talk with crowds and keep your virtue,*
*Or walk with Kings- -nor lose the common touch,*
*If neither foes nor loving friends can hurt you,*
*If all men count with you, but none too much:*
*If you can fill the unforgiving minute*
*With sixty seconds' worth of distance run,*
*Yours is the Earth and everything that's in it,*
*And- -which is more- -you'll be a Man, my son!*
*Rudyard Kiplin 1895*

# AFTERWORD

You may like to visit John's website at www.wheresharry.com

There's lots of info regards his cats, friends and his first novel. Still available from Amazon, it is a lighthearted, suited to all age groups, work of fiction titled: In The Hollow of the White Hazel

If you find you like the website and would like John to build one for you, or for your business, you can contact him directly via the message box at the bottom of the sites main page. I'm sure he'll be more than happy to help.

Coming soon: From the Bishops to the Potteries.
(Subject to a late change of title)
A fictional novel aimed at a more adult audience chronicling the romantic events of a time travelling thief turned good, a mysterious slide projector and a narrowboat driving getaway driver. Coming by the Spring of 2022.

Printed in Great Britain
by Amazon